IMAGES OF
SHOW BUSINESS
FROM THE THEATRE MUSEUM, V&A

Show Business was the title of the first of a series of major exhibitions staged by the Theatre Museum at the Victoria and Albert Museum before opening in its own building – the converted Flower Market in Covent Garden. The aim of the exhibition was not only to demonstrate the Theatre Museum's concern with all the performing arts – theatre, opera, ballet, circus, music hall, variety and rock – but also to indicate the enormous diversity of its collections. So the images range from David Garrick to David Bowie, from Nijinsky to Maria Callas, from Sheridan's own manuscript of **The School for Scandal** to posters and programmes, costumes and set designs from the 18th century to the present day.

This book, **Images of Show Business,** is both a complete record of the exhibition and a valuable and informative treasury of images from four centuries of the performing arts throughout the world.

Dr James Fowler, the editor, is Assistant Keeper of the Theatre Museum. He and the research staff have been able to draw fully on the multifarious resources of the Museum in writing and compiling this magnificent volume.

Serge Diaghilev watching a performance
of the ballet *Le Chant du rossignol* from the
wings during the 1920s
Laura Knight
Charcoal 368 × 267 [S.460–1979]

IMAGES OF

SHOW
BUSINESS

FROM THE THEATRE MUSEUM, V&A

EDITED BY JAMES FOWLER

methuen

LONDON

First published in Great Britain in 1982
simultaneously as a hardback and a Methuen Paperback
by Methuen London Ltd, 11 New Fetter Lane, London EC4P 4EE

Copyright © 1982 by the Theatre Museum
Designed by Peter Bennett

Printed in Great Britain
by Hazell Watson & Viney Ltd, Aylesbury, Bucks

ISBN 0 413 39980 X (hardback)
ISBN 0 413 39990 7 (paperback)

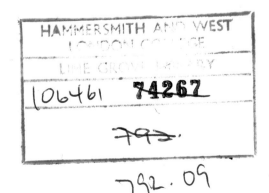

CONTENTS

Preface

Performers and Performances

1. Nijinsky
2. Andrew Ducrow/Florence Stephenson
3. Grisi and Lablache
4. The Beatles
5. Commedia dell'arte
6. Fred Astaire
7. Donald Wolfit
8. Kirsten Flagstad
9. Arthur Askey
10. Thomas Beecham
11. Sarah Siddons
12. *Salad Days/West Side Story*
13. Laurence Olivier
14. Negus the Lion
15. Noël Coward and Lilian Braithwaite
16. Marcel Marceau
17. Marie Taglioni
18. David Garrick
19. Barry Humphries
20. *She Stoops to Conquer*
21. George Leybourne
22. Edmund Kean
23. Charles Kean
24. Grimaldi
25. Sybil Thorndike
26. Isadora Duncan
27. Patti, Mario and Fauré
28. Charles Didelot
29. Paul Robeson and Peggy Ashcroft
30. David Bowie
31. Henry Irving
32. *Robinson Crusoe*
33. Margot Fonteyn
34. Peter Pears and Joan Cross
35. Music Hall: Novelty Acts
36. Circus: Aerial Acts
37. John Gielgud and Martita Hunt
38. Ellen Terry
39. Marie Callas
40. Deshayes and D'Egville
41. Sarah Bernhardt

42. Ivor Novello and Mary Ellis
43. Adolph Bolm
44. Caruso
45. Martha Graham/Janet Eilber
46. Musical Comedy: *The Arcadians*
47. Danny Kaye
48. Puppetry: *Starchild*
49. Dan Leno
50. Mick Jagger

Production processes
51. The Script: Author at Work
52. The Script: Censorship
53. Casting
54. Design Sketches: Messel
55. Costume Design: Anderson/W.S. Gilbert
56. Set Design: Parigi/Craig
57. Costume Design: Fedorovitch/Zinkeisen
58. Costumes: Circus/Pantomime
59. Set Design: Wakhevitch/Kenny
60. Costume Design: Erté/Fraser
61. Costume Design: Bianchini
62. Costumes: Musicals/Rock
63. Set Design: Léger/Piper
64. Costumes: Eighteenth Century/Nikolais
65. Set Design: de Loutherbourg/Butlin
66. Costume Design: Bakst
67. Set Design: Grieve/Caney
68. Costumes: Wilkinson/Sainthill
69. Scene Painting: Schervashidze, after Utrillo
70. Scene Painting
71. The Costumier
72. Properties
73. Prop-making
74. Rehearsals
75. Stage Lighting
76. The Dresser
77. Make-up
78. Backstage

Programmes, posters and publicity
79. Early Playbills
80. Early Illustrated Bills
81. Mid Nineteenth-century Bills
82. Late Nineteenth-century Poster: John Hassall
83. Early Twentieth-century Poster: Jean Cocteau
84. Modern Posters

85. Flyposting
86. Theatre Tickets
87. Satin Programme
88. Theatre Programmes: British
89. Poster Design
90. Theatre Programmes: International

Performance places

91. Pageant-wagons: the Ommeganck
92. Travelling Players: Piazza San Marco
93. Nouveau Elizabethan: Ashland, Oregon
94. Private Theatre of the Medici
95. Georgian Theatre: Richmond, Yorkshire
96. Edwardian Theatre: the Lyceum
97. Amphitheatres: Royal Amphitheatre / Astley's
98. Theatre-in-the-round: Royal Exchange
99. Performance-in-a-stadium: Wembley
100. Adaptable Theatre: the Octagon, Bolton
101. Place of Fun: the Pompidou Centre
102. Studio Theatre: the Gulbenkian, Newcastle
103. Travelling Theatre: the Bubble
104. Street Theatre: Covent Garden

Contributors

AS Alexander Schouvaloff
AT Anne Tuckwell
CEH Carolyn Harden
CH Catherine Haill
ER Eileen Robinson
DF Danny Friedman
JA Jennifer Aylmer
JF James Fowler
JS Janet Steen
SW Sarah Woodcock

All measurements are in millimetres, height before width

Acknowledgements

The authors wish to thank for their generous help:
Harriet Cruickshank, Royal Court Theatre, London; Ruth Eaton, *Northwich Guardian;*
Wendy Fisher; Chris Frampton; Margaret Harris; Janet Mein, Playhouse Theatrevan,
Harlow; Catherine Minshull; Dorothy Moore; Claire H. de Robilant; Sybil Rosenfeld;
Clare Street & Allan Bill Associates; Moira Walters; Priscilla Yates; Graham Brandon;
Vincent Burke, The Society of West End Theatre; Ian Callander, TBA Lighting; John
Cowell; John Crowe, The Playhouse, Harlow; Philip Dyer; Bob Fisher; Bob Gannon;
Ivor Guest; Peter Harlock, Royal Shakespeare Company; Nick Hern; Antony
Hippisley Coxe; Barry Humphries; Don Keller, National Theatre, London; Owen
Knowles, University of Hull; Gregor MacGregor, The Georgian Theatre, Richmond;
Cyril Mills; Michael Quine, The City University; David Scrase; Michael Sykes,
Wembley Stadium; Lyn Thomas; Simon Trussler; Bob Woodings; Box Office
Computer Systems, Space-Time Systems; British Theatre Association; Bubble
Theatre Company; Free Form Arts Trust Limited; London Festival Ballet; Octagon
Theatre, Bolton; Royal Exchange Theatre, Manchester.

The Theatre Museum is most grateful to the following for allowing copyright items
to be reproduced:
Jane Asher; Zoë Dominic; Chris Frampton, The Drawing Room; Carol Greunke;
Joan Hassall; Diana Seymour; Pennie Smith; Sheila Van Damm; Sarah Woodcock;
Doris Zinkeisen; Cyrus Andrews; Peter Barkworth; Clive Boursnell; Roger Butlin;
Reverend Cannon G. Carnes; H.E. Robert Craig; Anthony Crickmay; Robert Ellis;
Erté; Bob Gannon; Sir John Gielgud; Dezo Hoffman; Shuhei Iwamoto; Chris Madge;
Denis de Marney; David Oxtoby; John Piper; Donald Sinden; Barry Smith; Lord
Snowdon; John Timbers; Feliks Topolski; Georges Wakhevitch; Roger de Wolf;
David Wynne; Camera Press Ltd.; Crucible Theatre, Sheffield; Harvard Theatre
Collection; The Illustrated London News Picture Library; Keystone Press Agency
Ltd.; Macnaughton Lowe Representation Ltd.; Oregon Shakespearean Festival
Association; Messrs. Pettit & Westlake; Royal Court Theatre, London; Peter Saunders
Ltd.; Sotheby Parke Bernet & Co.; SPADEM; The Spotlight; Victoria and Albert
Museum; Winter & Kidson.

PREFACE

I t's easy to see what this book is about. You have only to flip through the pages to see the images which show the richness and scope of the collections which come from the Theatre Museum. The Theatre Museum is about live performance and all the means by which it happens. The objects in this book have been selected to help recapture and explain that elusive art and to act as an introduction to the Theatre Museum. There could have been many other selections. The objects were also chosen for an exhibition – the first of a series of three – at the Victoria and Albert Museum as a kind of *hors d'oeuvre* before the Museum opened in the Flower Market, Covent Garden in 1984.

In 1955 Laurence Irving wrote a letter to *The Times*. He suggested that there should be a theatre museum in England. Some ideas take longer than others to realize. It was not until 1974 that the Theatre Museum began. The site was fixed in 1975 and plans were drawn up. Final approval was given in 1979. And then in May this year came the recommendation to the Government that urgent consideration should be given to abandon the Museum. The fight was on. The Museum had to be saved. The intensity and vigour of the response to our appeal for help was so overwhelming and gratifying that on 11 August the Minister for the Arts announced that the Museum would go ahead as planned.

This book is dedicated to those Members of both Houses of Parliament who spoke for the Museum, to those who wrote letters not of condolence but of reasoned argument in its favour, to those journalists and broadcasters who persisted so enthusiastically with their campaign to save it, to all those who signed the petition in *The Standard* or the one David Hockney drew for the Theatre Museum Association, to the author of the recommendation because now more people know about the Theatre Museum than ever did before, and, in particular, to the following heroic friends: Lady St Just, Mrs Zoe Steadman, Mr Ian Armstrong, Mr Richard Buckle, Mr Richard Cave, Mr Richard Davies, Sir John Gielgud, Lord Harewood, Mr Antony Hippisley Coxe, Mr David Hockney, Lord Jenkins, Mr Louis Kirby, Mr Hugh Leggatt, Dr David Mayer, Lord Norwich, Mr Malcolm Pride, Sir Ralph Richardson, Mr Norman St John Stevas, Mr Milton Shulman, Mr Donald Sinden, Mr Angus Stirling, Smiley the Clown and his son, Mr David Vine and Mr Dylan Williams.

But this book is also dedicated to those who have generously given their treasured collections to the Museum because without them there would have been nothing to save, to Laurence Irving who inspired it all twenty seven years ago, and to all who work in the theatre.

Alexander Schouvaloff
Curator
15 August 1982

PERFORMERS
AND
PERFORMANCES

> But he, who *struts his hour upon the stage*,
> Can scarce extend his fame for half an age;
> Nor pen nor pencil can the Actor save,
> The art, and artist, share one common grave.

Few actors have expressed the ephemerality of their art more eloquently than David Garrick, who wrote these lines in his prologue to *The Clandestine Marriage* in 1766. And yet Garrick to us, unlike Thespis of Ancient Greece or Roscius of Rome, is more than just a name, thanks to those contemporaries whose pens and pencils captured the effect his acting made on them. Even if it had been possible to preserve Garrick's performances on film it would still be invaluable to know what impact he had on his audiences. In the age of video, reviewing has not been superseded as a record of performance, and performers continue to be the subjects of paintings, sketches, etchings, and bronzes. Fortunately, great actors, dancers, and singers have also set down what it feels like to them to perform.

Just before she took London by storm in the role of Isabella at Drury Lane in 1782, Mrs. Siddons was beset by 'the awful consciousness that one is the sole object of attention to that immense space, lined as it were, with human intellect from top to bottom, and all around, [that] may perhaps be imagined, but can never be described; and by me can never be forgotten'. However many times performers confront their audiences, the experience can still be the subject of dread, particularly as their reputation is almost always at stake. Laurence Olivier experienced uncharacteristic terror before his first-night appearance as Richard III at the New Theatre in 1944. For the first time in his life he felt incapable of learning his lines, and was convinced that it would be his worst performance ever. Yet he went on to give the first performance of what was to be one of his greatest roles.

Olivier's total involvement with his part is comparable with the attitude towards performing expressed by Margot Fonteyn in her autobiography: 'I cannot imagine feeling lackadaisical about a performance. I treat each encounter as a matter of life and death.' Lynn Seymour sums it up more directly still: 'If you can't be all concentration, physicality, joy, don't go on that fucking stage. . . . They want to see someone going on ready to die. It's thumbs up or thumbs down. Not a trick, no whoring, the real McCoy. You have to live dangerously on stage, otherwise it doesn't work'.

The first time Fonteyn saw Nureyev rehearsing she was struck by how absolutely seriously he practised – 'repeating every step with all his might until he almost knocked himself out with the effort. . . . So it went on for two hours. He was working like a steam engine.' And the choreographer Glen Tetley recalled of his early dancing career that the stamina required of him as a dancer exceeded that needed for his military training: 'I'd been through a tough commando course, but dance was far more difficult; the physical endurance seemed phenomenal.'

The physical strain of acting should not be underestimated, either. Actors and actresses are increasingly turning to work-outs as a means of coping with the physical demands made upon them. Lynn Redgrave puts strength, stamina, and good health even before talent among the qualities most necessary for a good actress: 'Acting is tiring; it requires a lot of work, a lot of muscle, an enormous amount of voice . . . you have to blow something up while making it look normal and do that for eight shows a week'.

Physical exercises form the basis of the intensive training actors undergo in the Theatre Laboratory run by the Polish director Jerzy Grotowski. Acrobatic skills are not acquired as ends in themselves but as a way of making the body the expressive instrument of spiritual qualities. The more intensive the actor's search for the inner self that must speak through his performance, the more rigorous the physical discipline for expressing it must be.

In his discussion of the theories of Artaud, Grotowski perceived an essential truth about acting –'that spontaneity and discipline, far from weakening each other, mutually reinforce themselves; that what is elementary feeds what is constructed and vice versa, to become the source of a kind of acting that glows'. The importance of achieving the right balance between the freedom and control emphasized by Grotowski is essential to a good performance: thus, Robert Tear speaks of the 'very piquant combination' of the excitement of letting himself go and yet remaining in control when singing.

If the artist is on form and the audience receptive, the shared experience can be exhilarating. Olivier describes such an occasion during the matinee following his début as Richard III: 'as I went on to the stage – the house was not even full – I felt this thing. I felt for the first time that the critics had approved, that the public had approved, and they had created a kind of grapevine, and that particular audience had felt impelled to come to see me. It was an overwhelming feeling, a head-reeling feeling, and it went straight to my head. I felt the feeling I'd never felt before, this complete confidence.'

If, on the other hand, the audience is unresponsive, the performer can be made uncomfortably aware of his isolation and vulnerability. Ken Dodd encountered a potentially disastrous situation at a Royal Variety Performance when he had to follow an act that had alienated the audience. As he told Michael Billington: 'All of a sudden a rod of steel entered my body and I thought You b————s. How dare you do this to me. I've been nearly twenty years in this profession, I've given my life to this profession. You're not going to do it. I brought every bit of courage from every corner of my body and every bit of skill I had acquired in Blackpool and Bournemouth and Scarborough and I thought I'll beat you or you'll have to come and shoot me before I go off. I worked and worked and worked on them and in the end I won.' It is the mark of a true professional to be able to rise to this kind of challenge.

Theatrical artists also have to deal with the problem of repeating a performance and 'bringing it off' every night. In 1980 David Bowie announced his decision to stop touring because he found three months of one-night-stands 'an extraordinary waste of time. The performance, I believe, becomes perfunctory after a bit. . . . The first two weeks have a great energy and drive, but after that one just waits for the end of the tour.'

Long runs can be a particular strain for actors. John Gielgud concedes that the discipline involved can be beneficial, but finds the routine of playing the same part eight times a week for more than a year nerve-racking –'agonizing work trying to keep one's performance fresh, without either slackening or over-acting'. And how to maintain the quality of a performance during a long run was a crucial problem for Stanislavski, who was fascinated by the capacity of great artists like Salvini, Duse, and Chaliapin to re-create their roles at every performance. Asking himself the question, 'Are there no technical means for the creation of the creative mood, so that inspiration may appear oftener than is its wont?', Stanislavski spent most of his life evolving a system of exercises to help the actor concentrate his whole being into a role and so throw himself 'into a part no matter what external obstacles may present themselves'.

Stanislavski must surely have approved of Richard Burbage, creator of Shakespeare's tragic roles, who remained 'in character' from the moment he dressed until the end of the performance – according to Richard Flecknoe in 1664, 'so wholly transforming himself into his part, and putting off himself with his clothes, as he never (not so much as in the tiring-house) assum'd himself again until the play was done'.

Whether an actor finds the role in himself or prefers to go beyond himself to become the character matters little. What counts, in Olivier's words, is the power of the actor to persuade 'himself, first, and through himself, the audience'. Or, as Sarah Bernhardt put it, how can the actor 'convince another of his emotion, of the sincerity of his passions, if he is unable to convince himself to the point of actually becoming the character that he has to impersonate'? This helps explain how some actors, such as Henry Irving in *The Bells* (see No. 31) can transmute inferior roles into great performances through force of personality and imagination.

What do audiences demand – and get – from the charismatic performers they champion? Maybe, as the American musical singer Stephanie Mills said of Barbra Streisand and Diana Ross, 'They have something that no one else has: it's unique, and it's a giving thing. It's strength. You look for that strength in them. That's what people come to see; they leave their frustrations and their problems at home and they look to the star for strength. That's what I do. It inspires you to keep going, keep dreaming, keep living.' *(JF)*

... the vivid, radiant boy is also the hierophant of mysteries, and in the glamour of his presence *Armide* comes to seem not merely a matchless display of lovely form in lovely motion, but also a type of the supreme functioning of a state of being most strange and utterly alien from our own.

GEOFFREY WHITWORTH (**THE ART OF NIJINSKY**, 1913)

The role of the favourite slave was written into *Le Pavillon d'Armide* by its choreographer Michel Fokine to show off the special qualities of Vaslav Nijinsky, most extraordinary of all the dancers recruited by Diaghilev for his first sensational Paris season of 1909. Dressed in a white, yellow, and silver costume trimmed with silk, lace, and ermine, with a jewelled band round the throat and wearing a white silk turban (now in the Theatre Museum), Nijinsky's first appearance was in a *pas de trois* with Tamara Karsavina and Alexandra Baldina. At the conclusion of the dance, excited by the audience's obvious admiration, he chose to leap off instead of adopting the simple walk-off demanded by the choreography – a jump so perfectly positioned that, as he reached the wings, he was still travelling upwards, and no one in the audience saw him begin to descend. His ensuing solo was designed to reveal his extraordinary lightness and virtuosity, and met with a buzz of admiration from the audience which culminated in wild cheering as he finished. That night the Nijinsky legend was born. He became the darling of the chic Paris audience, and the jewelled band he wore that night was so admired that it set a new fashion for chokers of black *moiré* set with jewels.

The photograph captures the fey quality and the characteristic turn of the head and unorthodox arm movements that were a hallmark of Nijinsky's style – while the legs, short and over-muscled, were the foundation of the legendary elevation. To his teachers at the Imperial School in St. Petersburg he seemed a brilliant technician, but did not fit into the conventional idea of the ideal male dancer. But Diaghilev perceived Nijinsky's true personality beneath the unprepossessing surface, and the choreographer Fokine enshrined his qualities in a series of roles in which he has never been surpassed: the mischievous Harlequin of *Carnaval*, the tormented puppet in *Petrushka*, the drifting spirit of *Le Spectre de la rose*, the animal Golden Slave in *Schéhérazade*. Subsequent generations have seen him as a mixture of the androgynous Spirit of the Rose, and the tragically inarticulate puppet Petrushka, fighting for his own individuality against an all-powerful master. *(SW)*

Vaslav Nijinsky (1888/9–1950), Russian dancer who quickly came to prominence after joining the Maryinsky Theatre, St. Petersburg, in 1907. In 1911, when Diaghilev established his company on a permanent basis with Nijinsky as star, he encouraged him to become a choreographer, and in such ballets as *L'Après-midi d'un faune* (1912), *Jeux*, and *Le Sacre du printemps* (1913), Nijinsky broke with pure dance traditions. His marriage in 1913 caused Diaghilev to dismiss him from the company. Later attempts to set up his own company failed, and by 1919 he had become irrevocably mentally ill, never to dance again.

Vaslav Nijinsky as Armide's Slave in *Le Pavillon d'Armide*, 1911
Photograph by de Meyer
London Archives of the Dance

He is the first true horseman that ever gave a meaning to the display of fine riding. He shows the attitudes of the ancient statues; – represents a peasant going to the fields to reap – getting weary – remembering an appointment with his mistress – and hastening to see her, until he seems breathless with his flight! – All this you see distinctly, although he is standing on a horse at full speed, the whole time.

LONDON MAGAZINE, AUGUST 1824 (AS QUOTED IN A. H. SAXON,
THE LIFE AND ART OF ANDREW DUCROW, 1978)

Circus as the English know it began with the horse. In 1768 an English ex-soldier, Philip Astley, began to put on equestrian shows in London and within a few years built what later became known as Astley's Amphitheatre. In time many itinerant acts – jugglers, animal acts, acrobats, clowns – came to perform at his theatre, and from these beginnings emerged the touring circus.

It was Astley who established the circus ring as 42ft in diameter, which remains the optimum size for riders to turn the effects of centrifugal force to best advantage.

The greatest equestrian star after Astley himself was Andrew Ducrow, and under his management in the 1830s Astley's knew its greatest days. Ducrow danced on horseback, performing acrobatics and combining brilliant horsemanship with theatrical roles. Nicknamed the 'Kean of the Circle', he appeared in costume appropriate to the characters featured in his many 'pantomimes on horseback', which included *The Roman Gladiator, The Chinese Enchanter, The Vicissitudes of a Tar*, and his most famous act of all, *The Courier of St. Petersburg. The Yorkshire Sportsman* (opposite) involved riding and leaping two bare-backed horses over a five-barred gate. It was first performed at Astley's in 1826, and this drawing was reproduced on Astley's bills advertising the act in 1830.

Ducrow was born and bred in the circus, as was Florence Stephenson, one of the Transfield family. In the late 1940s she and her sister Diana, displaying traditional circus versatility, claimed between them experience in wire-walking, trapeze, acrobatics, juggling, riding, and working a dog act. Here Florence is seen as a bare-back rider. The form of the act is traditional – the rosin back (as the horses are called, after the resin that is sprinkled on them to give the rider a better grip) canters round the ring and the rider negotiates a series of obstacles, leaping over ribbons or flags and through hoops. Indeed, so familiar has the act become that the glamorous lady bare-back rider, with her traditional ballerina skirt and shoes, has come to stand as a symbol of the spirit of the circus. *(SW)*

Andrew Ducrow (1793–1842), English equestrian, who in 1814 won acclaim as an actor in melodrama at the Royal Circus, and after touring the Continent from 1818 to 1823 returned to England and made débuts at Covent Garden and Drury Lane. He began his famous management of Astley's in 1825, performing there until it burnt down in 1841.

Florence Stephenson (b. 1929), English equestrienne, who appeared with Bertram Mills' Circus at Olympia in 1947–48 in the family wire-walking and dog acts, returning in 1948–49 with a 'Football Dogs' act (with her sister Diana) and her own 'Ballerina' act.

Andrew Ducrow enacting *The Yorkshire Sportsman or British Fox-Hunter, c.* 1830
William Heath
Pencil and watercolour 199 × 248 [S.134–1977]

Florence Stephenson with **Jeff** performing at Bertram Mills' Circus (Olympia, London, *c.* 1948)
Photograph by Baron Nicholas de Rakoczy

London was *steeped* in the music of *I puritani*; organs ground it, adventurous amateurs dared it, the singers themselves sang it to such satiety as to lose all consciousness of what they were engaged in, and, when once launched, to go on mechanically.

HENRY F. CHORLEY (**THIRTY YEARS' MUSICAL RECOLLECTIONS**, 1862)

Bellini composed the main roles of *I puritani* with four particular singers in mind – Grisi (soprano), Rubini (tenor), Tamburini (baritone) and Lablache (bass) despite the fact that a vocal quartet usually comprises soprano, alto, tenor and bass. Bellini was not disappointed by their performance at the Paris premiere (Théâtre-Italien, 24 January 1835): 'Lablache sang like a god, Grisi like a little angel, Rubini and Tamburini the same'. These singers, who became known as 'The Puritani Quartet', also sang the roles at the British premiere at the King's Theatre, 21 May 1835.

In the scene opposite, Elvira has just been told by Sir Giorgio Walton that he has persuaded her father to let her marry Arturo, the man of her choice. The hunting horns have just sounded the approach of Arturo.

'The Puritani Quartet' continued for several years, though Rubini was later replaced by Grisi's 'husband' Mario. Lablache and Grisi sang in many other roles together, and they were also linked by their connections with Princess Victoria. *I puritani* was her favourite opera, Grisi her favourite singer – and Lablache gave the Princess singing lessons. She was surprised that he did not share her views on Grisi, partly because the singer swallowed before a *roulade*, 'a habit she has contracted from fear of failing . . . I do not think he quite likes her'.

Lablache was the greatest singing-actor of his time, creating many roles, perhaps the most famous of which was the title role in Donizetti's opera *Don Pasquale*. But it was in *I puritani* that the unique qualities of four outstanding singers combined to make the opera an instantaneous success. As Bellini wrote: 'the opera, despite some uncertainty on the part of the chorus, had such a triumph, such enthusiasm, such a furor, that many people shouted, and never was so much applause recorded in a London theatre'. Young Princess Victoria was seen to clap her hands before anyone else. *I puritani* is still in the repertoire today, though it is not so frequently performed because of its strenuous demands on the singers. *(CEH)*

Giulia Grisi (1811–1869), Italian soprano best known for her Rossini and Donizetti roles, who made her début in the 1828–29 season in Bologna, and her London début as Rossini's Ninetta in *La gazza ladra* (King's Theatre, 1834), and frequently sang with the tenor Giovanni Mario, with whom she lived, before retiring in 1861.

Luigi Lablache (1794–1858), Italian bass, who made his La Scala début in Rossini's *La Cenerentola* in 1817, and sang in Vienna, Parma, London, and Paris. Particularly celebrated for his interpretation of comic roles, he retired in 1856.

Giulia Grisi as Elvira and **Luigi Lablache** as Sir
Georgio in *I puritani* (King's Theatre, London, 1835)
R. J. Lane after A. E. Chalon
Published by J. Mitchell, 1 January 1836
Lithograph coloured by hand 345 × 242
Harry R. Beard Theatre Collection. f.3–3

YEAH! YEAH! YEAH!
You have to be a real sour square not to love the nutty, noisy, happy handsome Beatles.
If they don't sweep your blues away – **brother, you're a lost cause.** If they don't put a beat in your feet – **sister, you're not living.**

DAILY MIRROR, NOVEMBER 1963 (QUOTED IN MICHAEL BRAUN,
LOVE ME DO: THE BEATLES' PROGRESS, 1964)

In a few short years The Beatles redefined popular music, transcending age, class, and cultural background with a sound that was firmly based in rock 'n' roll and yet was unique. Although they had been playing together in their native Liverpool since 1956, stylistically their watershed was Hamburg in 1960, where, as the Silver Beatles, they played eight-hour sets on orange-box stages with primitive equipment, learning to perform fast, loud, rhythmic rock 'n' roll and to 'mak show' as the Germans put it – rolling on the stage and generally acting their hearts out.

The Beatles brought their Hamburg incandescence back to the English stage, where their combination of harmony and attack, humour and harshness, naivety and guts was in startling contrast to the tedium extruded from the hit parade. The photograph of The Beatles opposite, at the Northwich Memorial Hall in the summer of 1963, catches their smartened-up image just at the time when Beatlemania was beginning to sweep the country.

Throughout the 1960s, The Beatles constantly reinterpreted pop. Though many bands, such as The Rolling Stones, reacted against the eclecticism of The Beatles's style, as Greil Marcus puts it, 'there was no possibility of a Left until the Beatles created the Centre'. In their day, The Beatles achieved a rapport with an immense audience that was a reflection of their own internal balance, and those who grew up in the 1960s could not but feel this unity – reflected here in Langdon Winner's words from the summer of 1967: 'The closest western civilization has come to unity since the Congress of Vienna in 1815 was the week the "Sgt. Pepper" album was released. . . . For a brief while the irreparably fragmented consciousness of the West was unified, at least in the minds of the young'. *(DF)*

The Beatles, English group who after the release of 'Let It Be' in 1970 broke up in a welter of personal and legal recrimination. **John Lennon** (1940–1980), with Yoko Ono, produced the most powerful music of the post-Beatles era such as on 'Imagine' (1971) and 'Mind Games' (1972), drawing heavily on commitments as diverse as the peace movement and Janovian therapy. **Paul McCartney** (b. 1942), with his wife Linda Eastman, formed the group Wings in 1971, producing a long series of commercially successful albums, notably 'Band on the Run' (1973), and singles such as the ubiquitous 'Mull of Kintyre'. **Ringo Starr** [Richard Starkey] (b. 1940) gradually diversified his career, moving from a number of jolly singles and albums through flirtation with furniture design to his more recent interest in acting and directing films. **George Harrison** (b. 1943) continued his interest in things eastern and experimental, as in his album 'All Things Must Pass' (1970), and has produced and arranged on his 'Dark Horse' label.

The Beatles: John Lennon, Paul McCartney, Ringo Starr and George Harrison
at work with George Martin at EMI's Abbey Road
studios, London, *c.* December 1963
Photograph by Dezo Hoffman

in performance at the Memorial Hall, Northwich,
Cheshire, July 1963
Snapshot by Bob Gannon
Given by the photographer

Rascals and acrobats ... perform improvised plays in the public squares, mangling the plots, speaking all off the point, gesticulating like madmen, and – what is worse – indulging in countless obscenities and vulgarities.

ANDREA PERRUCCI (**DELL'ARTE RAPPRESENTATIVA**, 1699)

Commedia dell'arte players emerged from the fairs and festivals of the rural districts of Italy in the sixteenth century. Famed for their improvised acting based on traditional scenarios, they were equally skilled at dancing, mime, singing, and acrobatics. Travelling from town to town in troupes, they carried with them a portable stage which they set up in the piazzas and on which they erected a curtained-off booth at the back (a similar commedia stage of a later date is featured as No. 92).

Jacques Callot (1592–1635) ran away from Nancy in northern France at the age of twelve, joined a commedia troupe, and travelled with them to Florence. His first-hand experiences inspired the lively detail of his set of etchings of the *Balli di Sfessania*, possibly associated with the festival of St. Stephen. How far the vignettes opposite reflect an actual scenario is uncertain, for it is difficult to determine whether the dancing and sword-play are part of the action on stage or are interludes in it.

These images include the escapades of two stock characters, the Captain and Pulcinella. The Spanish Captain is said to derive from the Italian hatred of the Spanish mercenaries on their soil, and his distinctive mask with curling mustachios, the cloak which he flourishes in the air, his rusty sword, and the defiant feathers in his cap typify the braggart soldier who is really a coward. If an actor excelled in the role his name became associated with it, hence the five named 'Capitanos' depicted here: Razullo and Cucurucu (e), Cap. Cardoni and Maramao (f), and Taglia Cantoni (c).

Though the stock character of the foolish servant is as old as farce itself, the Pulcinella of commedia was first closely associated with the actor Silvio Fiorillo. With typical commedia spontaneity he distinguished the character with a loose, large-buttoned tunic, belted pouch, baggy trousers, large peaked hat, and wooden sword.

Of the female roles illustrated here, Lucretia (b) was a famous 'Inamorata', or young lover, who wore everyday clothes, was unmasked, and not regarded as a comic character. Many women who played this role were accomplished singers and dancers and became famous in their own right as verse or scenario writers. Fracischina (a) was a maid-servant equivalent to the *zanni* manservant. She too wore everyday dress and no mask, but played an important comic role as intermediary for the lovers: extremely nimble and adept at disguise, sometimes as a young man in mistaken-identity situations, she could sing, dance, and accompany herself on the lute or tambourine as illustrated here. *(JS)*

a

Fracischina.   *Gian Farina.*

b

Pulliciniello.   *Sig.ª Lucretia.*

c

Taglia Cantoni.   *Fracasso.*

d

lucia mia.   *Berneualla.*   *Che buona mi s.*

BALLI DI SFESSANIA
di Jacomo Callot

Jac Callot In. fe.

e

Razullo.   *Cucurucu.*

f

Cap. Cardoni.   *Maramao.*

Commedia dell'arte characters.
Plates from a set of 24 entitled 'Balli di Sfessania', *c.* 1622
Jacques Callot
Etchings, each 72 × 90
Harry R. Beard Theatre Collection. Q.24

Ballet is the finest training a dancer can get and I had some of it, as a child. But I never cared for it as applied to me. I wanted to do all my dancing my own way, in a sort of outlaw style.

FRED ASTAIRE (**STEPS IN TIME,** 1959)

Fred Astaire was celebrating nearly 25 years on stage when he appeared in the Cole Porter musical comedy *The Gay Divorce* in 1933 – and for the first time he was working without his sister Adele, who had got married and left the stage the previous year. First as child stars on the American vaudeville circuit, then for sixteen years on the musical comedy stage, Adele had been the beauty, Fred the brains behind the novel dance routines that had dazzled audiences in New York and London.

His new leading lady was Claire Luce, and it was her style in *The Gay Divorce* that suggested to him the pattern of the dance to the hit song of the show, 'Night and Day'. This marked something new in musical comedy, and indeed in Astaire's career: the dance used as love duet. Playing a romantic lead for the first time, though lacking conventional good looks, Astaire found a way to create a unique romantic image in which emotion was expressed through movement instead of words. He was the perfect partner – at one with the girl's body, mirroring her line, enhancing her particular qualities, her vulnerable femininity emphasized by his unobtrusive sexuality.

Even motionless, Astaire is obviously a dancer, charged with energy and implicit movement, every part of the body consciously yet casually placed down to the fingertips, and totally harmonious: with Astaire, the transition from repose to movement, from movement to dance, is seamless. It was this tension of opposites that gave Astaire's work its special excitement – the calm surface overlaying unbounded energy, a freedom achieved through discipline, an insolent elegance.

During the London run of *The Gay Divorce* his first major film, *Flying Down to Rio*, was released in America, and Astaire's dancing of 'The Carioca' with Ginger Rogers proved a sensation. Astaire returned to America to find himself a film star, and never appeared in a full stage show again. *(SW)*

Fred Astaire [Frederick Austerlitz] (b. 1899), American actor and dancer who, on leaving the stage, became one of the most successful film stars of his time, notably in a series of specially written musical films with Ginger Rogers as his co-star – *Top Hat* (1935), *Swing Time* (1936), *Follow the Fleet* (1936) – until the partnership broke up in 1939. His later partners included Eleanor Powell, Rita Hayworth, Judy Garland, Cyd Charisse, and Leslie Caron. Regarded by many as one of the greatest dancers of the twentieth century, Astaire had no less reputation as a singer with many standards by Berlin, Kern, and Schwartz, written for him, including 'Cheek to Cheek', 'One for My Baby', 'The Way You Look Tonight', and 'Night and Day'.

Fred Astaire with **Claire Luce** dancing 'Night and Day'
in *The Gay Divorce* (Palace Theatre, London, 1933)
Photograph by Houston Rogers
Houston Rogers Collection

One could feel, as the poet means us to feel, that the great earth itself must tremble at his shaking. In all my mature experience I have not been so forced to forget all knowledge of Shakespeare and the theatre and live the action being performed. If this was not great acting, then I do not know where it can be found.

G. WILSON KNIGHT (**SHAKESPEARIAN PRODUCTION**, 1964)

Donald Wolfit was a great outsider of twentieth-century English theatre, an actor-manager of the old school in an age when even star players were submitting to the director and the ideal of ensemble playing. Wolfit preferred the life of an itinerant actor as the star of a vagabond troupe that took Shakespeare the length and breadth of the country – and did not too often venture into London. Thus, Wolfit built up his conception of King Lear for over two years before presenting the play in London in 1944.

The public showed little advance interest, but a half-full house on the first night greeted him with a storm of applause that, according to Beverley Baxter, 'ended in cheering as vociferous as if it had been the ballet or a football match'. The most influential critic of the day, James Agate, called it the greatest piece of Shakespearian acting he had seen, and suggested that Wolfit would be the natural leader of any National Theatre company, while C. B. Cochran claimed he had seen no greater actor since Irving. Edith and Osbert Sitwell told Wolfit: 'The cosmic grandeur of your King Lear left us unable to speak'.

Wolfit made no attempt to rationalize Lear's initial actions, nor to diminish the king to the level of an ordinary man. He was not afraid of the theatricality of the part, and in his mad scenes he not only challenged the storm but became the storm itself. He found the key to the character in Lear's unpredictability, and laid the seeds of the King's madness in the instability of an old man's passions – wilful, stubborn, proud, then wheedling, pathetic, cajoling – the moods ranging from towering anger to whining self-pity. McBean's photograph captures the Lear of the storm – broken, mad, afraid of the storm he has unleashed within himself and the enormity of what his own passions have created. As Edith Sitwell summed up the achievement, 'All imaginable fires of agony and all the light of redemption are there'. *(SW)*

Donald Wolfit [Woolfitt] (1902–1968), English actor and manager who made his stage début in 1920 and served a long apprenticeship on tour and in London at the Old Vic before taking leading parts at Stratford-upon-Avon in 1936, and in 1937 forming his own Shakespearian company. While his style came to appear old-fashioned to a new generation, he triumphed as Lear and Volpone, and after foreign tours for ENSA and on his own behalf in New York and Canada he briefly rejoined the Old Vic company in 1951 to win acclaim as Marlowe's Tamburlaine before resuming an independent career. He was knighted in 1957.

Donald Wolfit as King Lear
Photograph by Angus McBean

In studying and singing Isolde my back had developed so tremendously from all
the heavy breathing that my dresses actually burst apart.... Mind you, I
had not put on any additional weight. My lungs had expanded so.

KIRSTEN FLAGSTAD TO LOUIS BIANCOLLI (FROM **THE FLAGSTAD MANUSCRIPT,** 1953)

Kirsten Flagstad sang Isolde 182 times – as she put it herself, 'enough Isoldes for
one lifetime'. She first took the role at the National Theatre, Oslo, in 1932
and, following her début at the Metropolitan Opera, New York, as Sieglinde
in 1935, followed this with Isolde in a performance described by *The New
York Tribune* as 'a transcendently beautiful and moving impersonation'. English critics,
too, praised her performance in 1948, but for many, she was not the ideal Isolde, and
much as she loved the role, especially in the first act, she herself thought that 'neither
her voice nor personality was really right for Isolde, since the delineation of unbridled
sex is quite outside its range'.

In the quick sketch opposite, done direct from the stage, Topolski (b. 1907) captures
Flagstad in one of the most famous operatic love scenes. According to Wagner, Isolde
and Tristan are destined for each other.and already in love. The physical barriers to
their love must be removed. Considering herself betrayed, Isolde offers Tristan what
she believes to be a death potion – and he accepts, knowing it for what it is. Unknown
to her, her maid has substituted the love potion, and this breaks down all possible
resistance to a passion so great that it can only be tragically fulfilled through death.

After the war, Kirsten Flagstad was suspected by some of having Nazi sympathies
and suffered from picketing and riots at her performances in America. She sang on
regardless, and all accounts show her to have been a woman of courage and simplicity
with a voice of heroic standards, coupled with sound musicianship. Karl Rankl considered her the conductor's 'answer to all his prayers' for the unfailing strength and
beauty of her voice. *(CEH)*

Kirsten Flagstad (1895–1962), Norwegian soprano who made her stage début as
Nuri in d'Albert's *Tiefland* (Oslo, 1913). During the next eighteen years she sang a wide
range of roles in Scandinavia. Her first Isolde in Oslo in 1932 led to small parts at the
Bayreuth Festival the following year, and she became internationally renowned for
Wagnerian roles after appearing at the Metropolitan Opera, New York. Following her
retirement she became director of the Norwegian State Opera from its foundation in
1958 until 1960.

Kirsten Flagstad as Isolde and **August Seider** as
Tristan in *Tristan and Isolde*
(Royal Opera House, Covent Garden, 1948)
Feliks Topolski
Pen and ink 357 × 254
Given by the artist [S.148–1979]

> [Pantomime] is a great family affair and it's marvellous to hear the reactions from the kiddies. . . . Of course, in those days, the children were enchanted with the whole thing. . . . When I did my undressing scene as Dame, I used to get yells of laughter from the kids; now I remove my many petticoats to the accompaniment of wolf-whistles and cries of 'Get 'em off!'
>
> ARTHUR ASKEY (**BEFORE YOUR VERY EYES**, 1975)

Music-hall performers were imported into pantomime by Augustus Harris, manager of Drury Lane, during the 1880s, and by the turn of the century the dame tradition had reached its height in the work of Dan Leno (No. 49) and Herbert Campbell. It has continued through George Robey, Douglas Byng, Clarkson Rose, George Lacy – and Arthur Askey, who brings to the pantomime dame his comic *persona* 'Big Hearted Arthur', built up over years of playing in concert parties, in variety, and on radio and television. This he transfers directly into pantomime as Big Hearted Martha or Queen Martha or Nurse Martha, according to the dictates of the plot, together with a host of catch phrases instantly recognizable to two generations: 'Hello, playmates', 'Before your very eyes', 'Doesn't it make you want to spit?', 'Ithangyew'.

Despite the skirts imposed by the role, the projected image remains that of a mischievous, wickedly innocent schoolboy; his gusto and enthusiasm, and his love and enjoyment in performing, communicate immediately to his audience and this, combined with his natural gift for the ad lib, makes him an ideal pantomime performer, his neat, bespectacled, and 'whimsically roguish manner' recalling the family atmosphere of the seaside concert party in which he began his career.

If Arthur Askey himself was in the direct pantomime tradition, *Aladdin*, the Palladium pantomime of Christmas 1964, reflected a new trend. In the title role, the pretty female Principal Boy was banished in favour of a current teenage idol, and, as Harris almost a century before had brought music-hall stars into pantomime to keep it alive, so Bernard Delfont introduced pop star Cliff Richard and The Shadows to increase the appeal of his Christmas offering. But the pantomime dame continues to thrive, either in the traditional form, or with female impersonators like Danny la Rue, who emphasize not so much the comedy as the brilliance and glamour of the impersonation. *(SW)*

Arthur Askey (b. 1900), English comedian, who made his début as a concert artist in 1924, but whose great fame came through one of the first radio comedy series, *Band Waggon*, first broadcast in 1938. His highly successful career has embraced film, radio, and television and stage performances, notably in pantomime and summer seasons at the major venues.

Arthur Askey as Widow Twanky in *Aladdin and his*
Wonderful Lamp (London Palladium, December 1964)
Photograph by Cyrus Andrews
Showbiz Photo Collection

I have watched him draw flames, sighs, dreams, laughter out of them, and it is as though his spirit were reflected in a mirror that gives back his essence in thousandfold strength.

ETHEL SMYTH (QUOTED IN ALAN JEFFERSON, **SIR THOMAS BEECHAM,** 1979)

Thomas Beecham was a self-taught conductor who none the less became one of the first British conductors of international repute. He persuaded his wealthy father to bring the Diaghilev Ballets Russes to England in 1911, himself conducting for them, but he was rarely willing to make concessions to the dancers: later, in the 1930s, conducting for the Camargo Society, he took the Dance of the Cygnets from *Swan Lake* at about four times the normal speed, remarking with satisfaction, 'That made the b———s hop'.

As an impresario who was his own musical director, stage producer, and conductor in a world of increasing specialization, his multiplicity of talent came to be mistrusted, and his often irreverent approach to the music inevitably led to charges of amateurism and dilettantism. Unsurprisingly, Beecham was thus not invited to be involved in the establishment of an opera company at Covent Garden in 1947, even though he had been artistic director of his own seasons there from 1933 to 1939.

Beecham and Henry Wood were the first English conductors to aspire to the fame of the German stars like Bülow, Richter, Nikisch, and Weingartner. The conductors' names became as great a draw as the names of the great solo *virtuosi* or even the names of the composers on the programme. Beecham's temperament found a natural affinity with eighteenth-century music – especially Mozart, whose work he championed when it seemed it might be submerged beneath worship of Wagner. He was also the champion of Delius, introducing no less than four of Richard Strauss's operas to England, and many of Berlioz's lesser-known works. To eighteenth-century music he brought a unique perfection and subtlety of phrasing, a blending of grace and vitality, and all his conducting brought out his feel for classical form combined with a delight in sensuous colours and histrionics.

A feeling for drama in music made him an excellent opera conductor, though, paradoxically, he never cared for singers. Beecham's musical colleagues most truly discerned his qualities, none more clearly than fellow-conductor Malcolm Sargent who wrote: 'No conductor in my experience has shaped a melody with more tenderness and lustre of tone-quality and no one has been more diabolically shattering in moments of climax. On the rostrum he wove a hypnotic spell over both orchestra and audience'. *(SW)*

Thomas Beecham (1879–1961), English conductor and impresario, who successfully founded the Beecham Symphony Orchestra (1909), London Philharmonic (1932), Royal Philharmonic (1946), and the Beecham Opera Company (1915), the latter becoming the British National Opera Company in 1923. He was knighted in 1916 and made a Companion of Honour in 1957.

Thomas Beecham
David Wynne
Bronzes, 1958
S.284–1980 (Height 152)
S.285–1980 (Height 170)
S.286–1980 (Height 158)

> She embodied to our imagination the fables of mythology, of the heroic and the deified mortals of elder time. . . . Power was seated on her brow, passion emanated from her breast as from a shrine. She was tragedy personified.
>
> WILLIAM HAZLITT (**THE EXAMINER**, 16 JUNE 1816)

Sarah Siddons is the greatest tragic actress the English theatre has known. Yet her London début at Drury Lane in 1775 was a failure, and not until 1782 did she take the town by storm, playing the leading role in Southerne's *Isabella; or, The Fatal Marriage*. She consolidated her success with her interpretation of the role of Euphrasia in Arthur Murphy's ponderous classical tragedy *The Grecian Daughter*, as the devoted daughter who suckles her starving father, so preserving him to take his throne again after she has stabbed the usurper. The part had a strong appeal for Mrs. Siddons, and her interpretation combined filial devotion, joy, scorn, contempt, and heroic firmness – all very much to the taste of her audience.

The print illustrates the final moments of the play as Euphrasia stabs the tyrant Dionysius, who has usurped her father's throne and separated her from her infant son. In it can be glimpsed something of the towering grandeur of the Siddons style – a regal bearing, yet easy and graceful; the large expressive eyes that reflected every change of mood; and the flowing costume and close-cut hair which allowed nothing to distract from her facial expression. A monumental, statuesque quality was emphasized by sparing, carefully chosen gestures and the slowness of her speech.

Her command over her audience was complete. On stage she was possessed by the character she was playing, and even the other actors became choked with emotion in the face of her overpowering realism. Her audiences screamed, fainted, openly wept. Yet at the same time they could appreciate and savour the finer points of her virtuoso technique. Elderly playgoers long cherished the memory of her first entrance as Euphrasia, as she rushed onto the stage, veil streaming behind her, with the stirring cry of 'War on, ye heroes'– the spirit of Greece personified, raising the turgid verse almost to the level of great tragedy. *(SW)*

Sarah Siddons [née Kemble] (1755–1831), English actress, often acclaimed as the greatest tragedienne of the English stage. The sister of John Philip Kemble, she spent her childhood on tour with her father's theatrical company, and established her reputation in the provinces before achieving fame in London in 1782. Her other outstanding roles included Belvidera in Otway's *Venice Preserved*, Constance in *King John*, Jane Shore in Rowe's play, and, above all, Lady Macbeth – in which she bade farewell to the stage in 1812.

Sarah Siddons as Euphrasia in *The Grecian Daughter*
(Theatre Royal in Drury Lane, 1782)
C. Watson after R. E. Pine.
Published by J. Boydell, 1 May 1784
Mezzotint 518 × 403
Gabrielle Enthoven Collection

The kind of entertainment that demands an aura of benign tolerance usually associated with local productions organized by the vicar.

MILTON SHULMAN ON **SALAD DAYS** (**EVENING STANDARD,** 6 AUGUST 1954)

A total work that demands comparison not with musical comedy as we know it but with Menotti's operas or with *Porgy and Bess.*

J. R. ON **WEST SIDE STORY** (**MANCHESTER GUARDIAN,** 15 DECEMBER 1958)

When *Salad Days* achieved a London run of 2,283 performances, it had soundly beaten the records set by *Oklahoma!* and *Chu-Chin-Chow* as longest-running musical in London stage history. Originally planned as the 1953 Christmas production for the Bristol Old Vic, where Dorothy Reynolds – who co-wrote book and lyrics – was a company member, and composer Julian Slade musical director, *Salad Days* was first staged there in June 1954 before it transferred to London in August, performed by the Bristol Old Vic company, none of whom had special singing or dancing experience.

The fantasy plot, concerning a magic piano which makes everyone who hears it dance, was no more than a thread on which to hang a series of scenes that bore more relation to revue sketches than to an integrated musical plot of the kind established by *Oklahoma!* a decade before. But the 'artlessness' or 'amateurism' complained of by some critics was, in fact, carefully contrived by a team of young actors that, at Bristol, included Eric Porter, Alan Dobie, Pat Heywood, Dorothy Reynolds, Yvonne Coulette, and Norman Rossington, with Eleanor Drew and John Warner as the young lovers.

Salad Days had been running in London for four years when *West Side Story* hit the West End in December 1958. Devised by choreographer Jerome Robbins, *West Side Story* was an adaptation of *Romeo and Juliet* with the Montagues and Capulets translated into the warring street gangs of New York's West Side. Robbins's collaborators were some of the most formidable talents in New York theatre: composer Leonard Bernstein, designers Oliver Smith and Irene Sharaff, and, as lyricist, the young Stephen Sondheim. *West Side Story* demanded that specifically American breed of performer, 'a total artist whose role is so conceived that dancing (whether "dancing" or just "moving") is inseparable from singing and acting. At the top, choreographer and director became one' (Peter Brinson).

While critics of *Salad Days* made slighting comparisons with vicarage tea parties, *West Side Story* lent itself to articles in the press on 'Does Stage Violence Really Have so Serious an Effect on Children?'. But it could not equal the staying power of *Salad Days*, and chalked up a respectable but not outstanding 1,040 performances (though it was later to have a new lease of life as a film). Both musicals, however, had their champions and detractors – *The Times* called *Salad Days* 'a deep and refreshing draught from the fountain of youth', while Harold Hobson came up with the faint praise that *West Side Story* was 'a staggering *tour de force*, like *War and Peace* translated into Zulu'. *(SW)*

'Oh. Look at Me, I'm Dancing!' from *Salad Days*
Vaudeville Theatre, London, 1954
Photograph by Denis de Marney
British Theatre Museum Association

'The Rumble' from *West Side Story*
(Her Majesty's Theatre, London, 1958)
Photograph by Angus McBean

> When I first became a professional actor I lacked for food, I was hungry, out of work and terrified. . . . There's something about being brought up in an atmosphere of genteel poverty that makes you feel, 'I'll show them, I've got to show them'.
>
> LAURENCE OLIVIER (IN JUDITH COOK, **THE NATIONAL THEATRE,** 1976)

James Tyrone in Eugene O'Neill's *Long Day's Journey into Night* was in 1971 one of Laurence Olivier's last roles during his directorship of the National Theatre. Tyrone, based on O'Neill's own father, is an actor, successful in the eyes of the world, yet haunted by the spectre of the classical actor he could have become. A childhood of poverty has driven him to sell his artistic soul for the financial security offered by popular melodrama, but the memory of poverty and fear of its recurrence has turned him into a miser, while the miserliness has caused his wife's drug addiction and the alienation of his two sons.

Olivier gave a performance of great and thrilling complexity. He presented with understanding and sympathy a flawed, compelling human being, and through every action could be traced the past that formed the present man. It was the major achievement of Olivier's performance that behind the successful actor one could see the regret for the actor he might have been, behind the miser could be glimpsed the impoverished child. The fact that he was playing an actor allowed Olivier some magnificent moments of pure theatre, when it became increasingly difficult to disentangle James Tyrone 'acting' from Olivier seizing an opportunity for a display of theatrical virtuosity.

If there seemed an extraordinary bond of sympathy between Olivier and the role he was playing, this was, perhaps, because he too had known not only poverty, but the temptation of accepting the romantic type-casting of Hollywood as a straitjacket to his imagination. As an actor, he has always surrendered Laurence Olivier to the role, an approach often symbolized in the elaborate make-up which was the outward mask of the character within. But James Tyrone he played almost without make-up – and Olivier made his exit from the theatre in a major role bearing the soul of a character in whom he seemed to find direct echoes of his own. *(SW)*

Laurence Olivier (b. 1907), English actor, film star, director, and manager, who made his professional début in 1925, joined the Old Vic in 1935 to lay the foundations of his career as a classical actor, and achieved fame starring in Hollywood in films such as *Wuthering Heights* (1939) and *Pride and Prejudice* (1941). His own films of *Henry V* (1945) and *Hamlet* (1947–48) did much to popularize Shakespeare. In 1944 he became co-director of the Old Vic company at the New Theatre, and in 1957 moved into the new drama of the 1950s with his performance as Archie Rice in Osborne's *The Entertainer*. He was the first director of the National Theatre, 1963–74, since when his career has mainly been in films. Knighted in 1947, he became the first theatrical baron in 1970.

Laurence Olivier as James Tyrone in *Long Day's Journey into Night* (National Theatre at the New Theatre, London, 1971)
Photograph by Zoë Dominic

Lions and tigers are felines, hence all their life long are subject to the play-impulse. It is a good trainer's first duty to exploit this play-instinct, and the curiosity of the beasts. . . . All cats are vain and take pleasure – consciously or unconsciously – in graceful poses and elegant movements. That is the second point of departure for the trainer. The rest must be supplied altogether by him and by him alone – love, attention, care and observation, patience and fearlessness.

PAUL EIPPER (**CIRCUS: MEN, BEASTS, AND JOYS OF THE ROAD,** 1931)

Training animals for public show differs only in degree (and, sometimes, danger) from training any domestic animal. By specialized handling and continuous use of effective cues, a circus animal can be taught to perform certain actions at a special personal signal, the main principle being that 'animals are never forced to execute at the command and will of others any movements which are not natural to them in a free state' (Dr. H. Hediger). A trainer first observes his animals closely, to establish these movements and their individual qualities, before training can begin, and during this time familiarity of surroundings and the establishment of habit are of maximum importance in giving the animal security.

Most modern training follows the work of Carl Hagenbeck in the second half of the nineteenth century, and is based on an understanding of animal psychology allied to a humane approach. The trainer must, however, impose his will unequivocally because the animal would consider any indulgence as weakness, and this could have serious consequences.

Negus, the wire-walking lion, trained by Alex Kerr, appeared with Bertram Mills' Circus at Olympia in the 1950–51 Christmas season. Alex Kerr did not begin lion-training until 1949, but once accepted as a trainer he spent three or four weeks living with the lions night and day, looking after them and speaking to them in a peculiar mixture of German and his native Glaswegian dialect. In this way he accustomed them to his presence and familiarized himself with each animal's personality.

It took six months' patient graded training to perfect Negus's tight-rope walking act. The one-and-a-half-inch-thick cables were laid on the ground until Negus realized it did not hurt him to walk on them. Then day after day, tempted by pieces of meat, the lion learned to walk step by step across the ropes. Only then were they raised off the ground – first by six inches, then by two feet, and so on up to the final height of six feet. On the extreme right of the picture can be seen the trainer's stick, indicating to the lion the position of the next step, and it is on this that the animal's whole concentration is focused. *(SW)*

Negus performing with Bertram Mills' Circus
(Olympia, London, 1950–51)
Photograph by Baron Nicholas de Rakoczy

As an actor [Coward] was absolutely in the front. He could play these nervous strange people, hysterical people, which is very rare. . . . And it's only people who are hysterical who can play hysterical parts. He was absolutely wonderful. You see, he could *scream!*

SYBIL THORNDIKE (QUOTED IN **NOËL** BY CHARLES CASTLE, 1972)

By 1924 Noël Coward was already known as author, composer, and lyricist of a revue, *London Calling*, but it was *The Vortex* that established him as an actor; indeed his original motive had been 'to write a good play with a whacking great part in it for myself'. That part was Nicky Lancaster, the drug-taking son of Florence Lancaster, an ageing society beauty who tries to stave off the ravages of time by taking lovers from among her son's friends. The production at the Everyman Theatre, Hampstead was fraught with difficulties, which culminated in the resignation of Kate Cutler who was playing Florence, and who was replaced by Lilian Braithwaite only a week before the first night.

The climax of the play comes in the last-act confrontation, in which Nicky forces his mother to accept her age, his drug addiction, and her own maternal role. On the first night, tense with his responsibilities as playwright, actor, and director, Coward gave a magnificent *tour de force* of nervous, hysterical acting, while Lilian Braithwaite astounded the critics by 'completely transforming herself, both physically and temperamentally, into a worthless baggage of modern woman'. The play scandalized the theatrical establishment, and the words 'filth', 'decadence', and 'dustbins' were bandied about. To the young, however, it came as a revelation: Nicky Lancaster became a symbol of 1920s youth much as Jimmy Porter was to become a symbol of 1950s youth in *Look Back in Anger*. As Coward had hoped, the play established him as a serious dramatist, while the surrounding scandal was good for business: the play thus successfully transferred from the Everyman, Hampstead, to the West End, where it ran for over a year with John Gielgud taking over the role of Nicky when Coward left the cast. From then on, as Coward observed, 'Success took me to her bosom like a maternal boa constrictor'. *(SW)*

Noël Coward (1899–1973), English actor, dramatist, composer, and director, who became regarded as the *enfant terrible* of the 1920s English theatre, and developed as a writer of musicals with *Bitter Sweet* (1929) and *Cavalcade* (1931). Among his successful plays were *Hay Fever* (1925), *Private Lives* (1930), *Design for Living* (1932), and *Blithe Spirit* (1941). He was knighted in 1970.

Lilian Braithwaite (1873–1948), English actress who made her professional début in Natal in 1897, and subsequently established herself as a distinguished actress in London with Julia Neilson in 1900, Frank Benson, and George Alexander at the St. James's. Her career took on new impetus after her performance as Florence Lancaster in *The Vortex*. She was created D.B.E. in 1943.

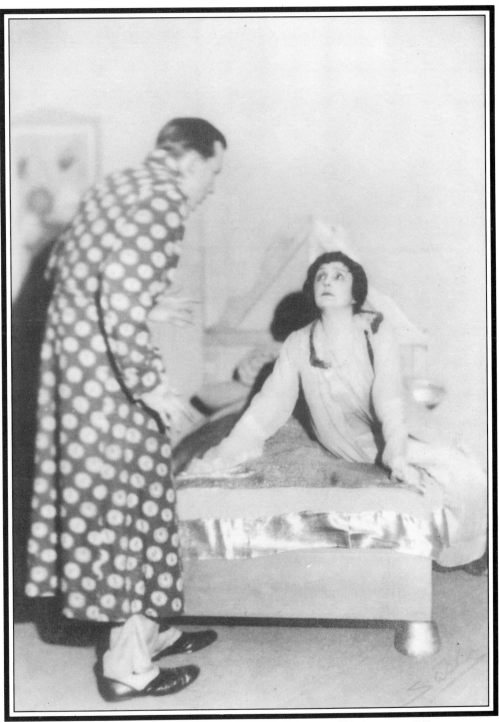

Noël Coward as Nicky Lancaster and **Lilian Braithwaite** as Florence Lancaster in *The Vortex*, 1924
Photograph by Sasha

I want to use the theatre with the freedom of the painter or the film maker. A theatre that cannot make people wonder is no theatre for me. We have to try to do things nobody else can do. I want to be a god on the stage.

MARCEL MARCEAU (IN INTERVIEW WITH FRANK MARCUS, 1962)

In the performance illustrated here, Marcel Marceau enacts the planting of a seed which he watches grow taller and taller until it bursts into flower and is visited by a bee. The image catches him in a moment of wonder, akin to fear, as he becomes both rapt onlooker and creator of the mystery of growth. In his utter involvement in his action he synthesizes imagination and reality: his hand *is* the flower and his face expresses his emotion. A black-and-white photograph such as this – taken at a photocall session during Marceau's 1978 visit to Sadler's Wells – is a particularly appropriate medium in which to express the starkness and isolation of Marceau's actions on stage, and the combination of his black costume and whitened face intensifies one's concentration on the hands and face which are telling the story.

Whilst Marceau claims to be directly descended from the fools and mime-artists of Graeco-Roman times, he lies firmly in the great French mime tradition awakened in Paris in the 1820s by Deburau, who played the sad white-faced pierrot in the Funambules pantomime theatre. In 1944 Marcel Marceau, then a pupil of the actor-manager Charles Dullin, saw the art of the legendary Deburau re-enacted by Jean-Louis Barrault (like Marceau, taught by Etienne Decroux) in Marcel Carné's film, *Les Enfants du Paradis*, and, having admired from the beginning the silent clowns of the early cinema – Charlie Chaplin, Buster Keaton, Laurel and Hardy, and Harpo Marx – Marceau created the character of 'Bip' in the style of a Chaplinesque tramp-clown.

Marceau formed his own company which went on to tour the world, and was influenced in turn by Japanese Noh and Kabuki theatre and by Indian dance. Intent on passing on the circus and music-hall arts of clowning, and his manipulation of the human body to manifest emotion without words and 'make the invisible real', he opened in 1969 what is now the 'International School of Mimedrame Marcel Marceau' in Paris. But as Lindsay Kemp, a former student of Marceau, has remarked, there is a limit to which the art can be taught, and ultimately 'a great mime is'. *(AT)*

Marcel Marceau (b. 1923), French mime, who first appeared in London at the Arts Theatre in 1952 and has since gained an international reputation. In addition to the character Bip, he has created many mime pieces such as *The Overcoat* (1951), based on Gogol, and *Don Juan* (1964).

Marcel Marceau (Sadler's Wells Theatre, London, 1978)
Photograph by Shuhei Iwamoto

She floats like a blush of light before our eyes: we cannot perceive the subtle means by which she contrives, as it were, to disdain the earth, and to deliberate her charming motions in the air.

(**THE MONTHLY CHRONICLE,** JULY–DECEMBER, 1838)

The ballerina Marie Taglioni was at the height of her powers when this description appeared. With her the aspirations and ideals of the Romantic era entered the ballet and she became their tangible symbol. *Le Dieu et la Bayadère* (1830), the opera-ballet from which the one-act ballet *La Bayadère* was taken, came two years before *La Sylphide* crystallized the Romantic ballet style in dance, and made Taglioni the rage of the ballet world. As an opera-ballet, combining dance and song, its form was already old-fashioned when it was first performed in Paris in 1830, but its subject matter, taken from a poem by Goethe, fixed it firmly as a product of its era. It told of a bayadère (Indian temple dancer) whose unselfish devotion saves her from the funeral pyre and wins her immortality at the side of her lover, the god Brama – a far cry from the European mythology and pastoral subjects that provided the libretti for eighteenth-century ballet.

Looking at the lithograph of Taglioni in *La Bayadère* today, the pose seems conventional enough, but in 1830 it would have seemed intriguingly novel to most of her audience. Taglioni's lightness and ethereality were achieved by the exploitation of the most exciting and far-reaching development that dance had known for decades – the technique of dancing on the tips of the toes, in shoes which had no stiffening, save the careful darning of the tips (done by the dancer herself) which served to give added grip on the stage. The development of *pointe* work, and the consequent emphasis on the ballerina, combined with the idolization of Taglioni caused a reaction against the male dancer which persisted until the rise of Diaghilev.

A characteristic of the Romantic ballet lithograph is that it idealizes the subject, as in this work by A. E. Chalon (1780–1860) based on one of six portraits he made of Taglioni during her season at the King's Theatre in 1831. Taglioni was plain, with arms so long they almost constituted a deformity, and so round-shouldered that she was almost a hunchback, but her father, Filippo Taglioni, skilfully arranged his choreography to minimize these defects. So successful was he that the style of the ballets he created for her became the epitome of the Romantic ballet style, and a new word 'taglioniser' was created to define her new style of dancing. *(SW)*

Marie Taglioni (1804–1884), Swedish-Italian dancer, born in Stockholm, and acclaimed throughout Europe for her transformation of the dance by her artistic application of *pointe* work notably in *La Sylphide* (1832). The image of the ballerina with centre-parted hair and long soft dress emanates from her. She retired in 1847 and, after losing her fortune in 1870–71, taught dancing and deportment in London.

Marie Taglioni in the title role of *La Bayadère*
(King's Theatre, London, 1831)
R. J. Lane after A. E. Chalon.
Published by Ackermann and Co.
Lithograph coloured by hand 563 × 358
Marie Rambert-Ashley Dukes Collection [E.5046–1968]

In his face all can observe, without any great refinement of feature, the happy intellect in his unruffled brow, and the alert observer and wit in the lively eye, often bright with roguishness. His gestures are so clear and vivacious as to arouse in one similar emotions.

FROM GEORGE LICHTENBERG'S 'LETTER FROM ENGLAND', 1 OCTOBER 1775

Jean Fesch (*c.* 1738–1778), a Swiss miniaturist, may have met David Garrick on Garrick's Grand Tour of 1763–65. He followed the actor to London and prepared the miniatures for John Smith's *Dramatic Characters from the English Stage in the Days of Garrick* (1770). This miniature is very similar in style and is probably contemporary with the engravings in that work: it is here reproduced in colour for the first time.

Benedick was one of Garrick's favourite comic roles, in which he liked to make his first appearance of the season. He was famous for his extraordinary range of facial expression, but Fesch draws our attention to Garrick's mastery of gesture as a means of portraying character. This lively bow captures Benedick's dash and vigour and is delivered with the panache that must have won over Garrick's audiences. How Garrick achieved the effect is best explained by Lichtenberg: 'when he turns to some one with a bow, it is not merely that the head, the shoulders, the feet and arms, are engaged in this exercise, but that each member helps with great propriety to produce the demeanour most pleasing and appropriate to the occasion'.

Lichtenberg goes on to remark how Garrick, despite being short and thick-set, had absolute physical control, which made his movements powerful and graceful at the same time: 'In the dance in *Much Ado About Nothing*, also, he excels all the rest by the agility of his springs; when I saw him in this dance, the audience was so much delighted with it that they had the impudence to cry "encore" to their Roscius'.

Garrick believed his interpretations could be enhanced by careful choice of costumes and he accordingly spent considerable sums on them, aiming rather for theatrical effect than strict historical accuracy. Here, the brilliant red coat trimmed with gold emphasizes Benedick's flamboyant nature. It also corresponds closely to an army officer's uniform of Garrick's day, with its gold epaulet on one shoulder, and small black bow on the tricorne hat, so apt for Shakespeare's 'good soldier'. *(JS)*

David Garrick (1717–1779), English actor, manager, and dramatist, who took London by storm as Richard III in 1741. His more natural style of acting helped overturn the declamatory manner of James Quin, whom he far excelled in great tragic parts such as Macbeth, Hamlet, and Lear. Garrick also played comic roles, including Benedick, Abel Drugger in Jonson's *The Alchemist*, and Bayes in Buckingham's *The Rehearsal* with equal success. During his management of Drury Lane from 1747 until his retirement in 1776, Garrick improved costume, scenery, and lighting and rid the stage of unwanted spectators.

Mr GARRICK *in* **BENEDICT.**
in Much ado about nothing.

David Garrick as Benedick in *Much Ado About Nothing*,
c. 1770
Jean Louis Fesch
**Watercolour, indian ink and gold paint on
vellum** 105 × 88 [S.446–1979]

> Performing exhilarates me, darlings. The adrenalin is pumping to every fibre and corner of my organism when I'm on stage.
>
> DAME EDNA EVERAGE, HOUSEWIFE SUPERSTAR, 1980

Dame Edna Everage, an ebullient and highly individual character created by Barry Humphries, was gracious enough to grant us this interview: 'I feel at home on the stage, oddly enough. I feel that it is my element, which is extraordinary considering I am an untrained actress. I didn't go to drama school, RADA, or any of these things. I have no diplomas but of course I have a Damehood. That's a good deal better than a lot of their measly documents, little bits of parchment and vellum. I have a Damehood for my services to Australian culture, and also because I'm Australia's answer to Vanessa Redgrave and Jane Fonda. Not that they're Dames, and not likely to be either.

'As for the acting part of it, it's not acting, you see, it is a sharing thing. I have the gift of instant communication. You can put my name up in lights in Piccadilly Circus, as it often has been, and the public of all nationalities will flock along. I think that's a sign, isn't it? A kind of magnetism.

'I give. I give so much. What star do you know, what artiste do you know, who gives so much as I do? I mean, there's a nominal charge to see my shows but most people think it's far too little. But I give gifts to the people I speak to in the audience and chat with. Some of them I have to be brutally frank with, particularly if they're dowdy old frumps. It's my duty to tell them so. They'll come back to see me again, because people like a bit of stick.

'I've always loved the gladdi because to me it expresses everything about our wonderful suburban way of life in Australia. I always fling them to the audience, and at every show I do I see grown men knocking over little old ladies, grabbing at the gladdies. I try to import them from Australia because people like a thicker stalk in their hands, generally speaking. I find the sturdier stalks appeal to a wider group of people.'

Barry Humphries (b. 1934), Australian actor, who appeared as Mr. Sowerberry in the original production of *Oliver!* (1960), returned to Australia in 1962 with his one-man show *A Nice Night's Entertainment*, and starred in the West End with Spike Milligan in *The Bed Sitting Room* (1963). He appeared in two of Joan Littlewood's productions and the Lionel Bart musical *Maggie May* (1964), and has written and played in two Australian films featuring the character Barry Mackenzie. His one-man shows in London include *Barry Humphries – Housewife Superstar* (1976), *A Night with Dame Edna* (1978), *The Last Night of the Poms* (1981), and *An Evening's Intercourse with Barry Humphries* (1982). *(CH)*

Barry Humphries as Dame Edna Everage in
An Evening's Intercourse with Barry Humphries
(Theatre Royal, Drury Lane, 1982)
Photograph by John Timbers

Marlow (Kneeling.) Does this look like security. Does this look like confidence.
No, Madam, every moment that shews me your merit, only serves to
encrease my diffidence and confusion . . .

OLIVER GOLDSMITH (**SHE STOOPS TO CONQUER**, ACT V, SCENE 3, 1773)

In this climactic scene from Goldsmith's *She Stoops to Conquer*, Kate Hardcastle, still
disguised as a serving-maid to test Charles Marlow's love for her, proves it to their
respective fathers by arranging a meeting within their hearing. Charles admits
his love for her, but stresses that he cannot possibly marry beneath him and must
therefore reluctantly take his leave. She reproves his easy confidence in winning her, at
which he kneels, protesting his sincerity. Charles's father emerges from behind the
screen, Kate's true identity is revealed, and her estimate of Marlow's fidelity is vindi-
cated – much to the young man's embarrassment.

Opposite is one of six paintings prepared by Francis Wheatley (1747–1801) for *Bell's
British Theatre* texts, and engraved and published as the frontispiece to the play in
December 1791. It is one of the earliest representations of the comedy, which has
remained a popular success since its first performance at Covent Garden on 15 March
1773. The softness of the colouring in the painting is more reminiscent of pastel than
oil, and may reflect the glow of candlelight which would have lit the scene in the
theatre. The melting quality also suggests the poignancy of the situation and the gentle
interplay of the characters.

The setting has a theatrical feel which tempts one to identify the figures with actual
performers – possibly John Barnard, Mrs. Mattocks, and James Fearon, who all
appeared together as Marlow, Kate, and Sir Charles at Covent Garden in 1788–89.
If these are the artists featured, Wheatley is more likely to have painted them in his
studio, according to the custom of the time, than in the theatre. Unfortunately there is
no firm evidence that he drew on a contemporary production of the play. *(JS)*

Charles Marlow and Kate Hardcastle, with their fathers
behind the screen in *She Stoops to Conquer*
Francis Wheatley
Oil on canvas *c.* 1790. Diameter 495
V & A: Department of Paintings,
given by F. J. Nettlefold [P.15–1947]

For Champagne Charlie is my name,
Champagne Charlie is my name
Good for any game at night, my boys,
Good for any game at night, my boys.
Champagne Charlie is my name,
Champagne Charlie is my name
Good for any game at night, my boys,
Who'll come and join me in a spree.

(LYRIC FROM THE ILLUSTRATED MUSIC COVER SHOWN OPPOSITE)

With this refrain George Leybourne established himself as one of the great music-hall stars. The image he set before his working-class audience was a caricature of the West End 'swell' of mid-Victorian London with his monocle and fashionable 'Dundreary' whiskers, gaily coloured waistcoat and trousers, and glistening boots. By 1865 he was a 'top liner' at the Canterbury Hall, Lambeth, at the then enormous salary of £30 a week, but 'Champagne Charlie' consolidated his success and his salary rocketed to £120.

Liquor manufacturers were not slow to seize upon the publicity value of 'Champagne Charlie', and Leybourne and The Great Vance embarked upon a profitable rivalry, pushing the merits of various intoxicating liquors –'Moët and Chandon's the Wine for Me'; 'Cool Burgundy Ben'; 'Sparkling Moselle'; and even the solid virtues of 'Our Glorious English Beer'. Other songs popularized by Leybourne included the respectable 'Up in a Balloon' and 'The Little Eel Pie Shop', and the less polite 'If Ever I Cease to Love' and 'They All Do It', which earned him several stern warnings from the law. But only one song other than 'Champagne Charlie' has survived him –'The Daring Young Man on the Flying Trapeze', in honour of Léotard.

In his gleaming top-hat and a great-coat with the largest fur collar in London, Leybourne became a strange mixture of a man-about-town and a Bohemian. His immense popularity led to engagement after engagement, often several in a night, and he spent his evenings dashing from hall to hall in a carriage drawn by the four white horses that had become one of his publicity gimmicks.

The illustrated music cover was another means of publicity seized on and exploited by the first generation of music-hall stars. Up to the 1860s sheet music publishers had relied upon imaginative and evocative pictures to sell their wares: now, a potent selling aid was to feature the star who made the song famous, and Leybourne was among the first to be featured in this way. Here he is enshrined in an image originally drawn in 1867 by Alfred Concanen (1835–1886), the great master of the illustrated music cover. *(SW)*

George Leybourne [Joe Saunders] (1842–1884), English music-hall performer, who was a mechanic before he appeared in the music-halls and free-and-easies of the Midlands and the North, making his London début in 1864. In later years he suffered from bad health and a decline in his popularity, and last appeared at the Queen's Theatre, Poplar, in 1884.

George Leybourne
Illustrated music cover
R. Childs after A. Concanen
Printed by Siebe and Burnett
Colour lithograph 343 × 224

Who that ever saw will ever forget the fascination of his dying eyes in Richard, when deprived of his sword; the wondrous power of his look seemed yet to avert the uplifted arm of Richmond.

FANNY KEMBLE (QUOTED IN W. CLARK RUSSELL, **REPRESENTATIVE ACTORS**)

The role of Richard III, with its violent energy and villainy heightened by Cibber (whose adaptation still kept Shakespeare's original from the stage), suited Edmund Kean perfectly, and his short stature became an asset rather than a liability. Kean was the embodiment of the Romantic era in acting, admired for the wild emotionalism of his performances – a passion and energy in marked contrast to the cold, statuesque formality of John Philip Kemble, who had dominated the stage in the early years of the nineteenth century.

Kean's acting appeared natural and unpremeditated; words and actions seemed to proceed from the inspiration of the moment, even though his effects had been meticulously planned. His expressive eyes, a voice soft in tenderness and harsh in violent passion, his energy and concentration – all gave him 'an entire mastery over his audience in all striking, sudden, impassioned passages, in fulfilling which he has contented himself, leaving unheeded what he could not compass – the unity of conception, the refinement of detail, and evenness of execution' (Fanny Kemble).

Kean's attitude was summed up in the instruction he sent to his fellow actors: 'Tell them to keep upstage of me and do their damn'dest'. His death scene as Richard III, illustrated opposite, was one of his most memorable achievements. 'He fought like one drunk with wounds', wrote Hazlitt, 'and the attitude in which he stands with his hands stretched out, after his sword is taken from him, had a preternatural and terrific grandeur, as if his will could not be disarmed, and the very phantoms of his despair had a withering power'.

Tinsel pictures were an elaboration of the theatrical prints which sold in their thousands in the early years of the nineteenth century. A basic black and white engraving was decorated with fabric, scraps of leather or feathers, tinsel armour, and dots and stars, until a 'collage' was produced, each one unique to the maker. However standard the poses in these prints, Kean's piercing eyes and intense expression would seem to approximate to his stage performance, and the simple, heroic pose here undoubtedly reflects current acting style. *(SW)*

Edmund Kean (1787–1833), English actor, whose fame dates from his début as Shylock at Drury Lane in 1814, when he established himself as the leading tragedian of his day. Besides Richard III and Shylock, his greatest interpretations included Sir Giles Overreach in Massinger's *A New Way to Pay Old Debts*, Barabas in Marlowe's *The Jew of Malta*, and Macbeth, but his talent dissipated itself in drink and high living, which helped to alienate him from his audiences and eventually led to his death.

Edmund Kean as Richard III with **John Cooper** as
Richmond (Theatre Royal, Drury Lane, November 1821)
Anonymous
Published by J. Fairburn, 1838
Etching, tinsel, and fabric appliqué
268 × 318 [E.114–1969]

The *Benedick* of Mr. C. Kean is decidedly the best on the stage. The soliloquy in which he discovers that 'the world must be peopled' was never better delivered. The smile that spreads over his face, and remains there illuminating the countenance for a while, reminds us strongly of Mr. Edmund Kean's peculiar fascinating geature, with which he so frequently contrived to irradiate his featural expression.

THE ILLUSTRATED LONDON NEWS, 27 NOVEMBER 1858

Son of Edmund Kean, but resembling him little in temperament or talent, Charles Kean's management of the Princess's Theatre between 1851 and 1859 was characterized by pedantic, historically accurate productions, especially of Shakespeare, which exactly hit the Victorian taste for the explicit combined with the picturesque.

Much Ado About Nothing (1858) was one of the last Shakespearian plays produced by Kean at the Princess's. Unusually for him, little was said on the playbill or in the printed text about the scenic effects and costumes and the historical research undertaken, but it appears from J. W. Cole's account of the production that no expense was spared on scenery or costumes: 'The opening view, the harbour of Messina, was quite a pictorial gem. The gradual illumination of the lighthouse and various mansions, in almost every window, the moon slowly rising and throwing her silver light upon the deep blue waters of the Mediterranean, were managed with imposing reality'. The masquerade scene, here shown in a bare photographer's studio, was set with 'variegated lamps, bridge, gardens, and lake, seen through the arches of the palace'.

Kean's productions were meticulously recorded in a series of watercolours. The 1850s also saw the growth of photography as a commercial proposition, and later Princess's productions were recorded by Laroche and issued in a series of stereoscopic photographs. The stereoscope was invented to re-create artificially the natural phenomena of binocular vision. Two photographs of the same scene are mounted side by side, each taken from a slightly different viewpoint corresponding to the left and right eye. When viewed through a binocular viewer a 3-dimensional effect is achieved. A stereoscopic camera, with two lenses set $2\frac{1}{2}$ inches apart, allows both photographs to be taken at once. The craze for stereoscopic pictures only died out with the development of the more manageable *carte-de-visite* prints in the 1860s. This photograph appears to be an enlargement of one of a stereoscopic pair which had been coloured by hand. Despite the long exposures required for the photography of the time the Keans convey surprising vitality.

Mrs. Kean's costume here remains suspiciously close to the fashionable crinoline, and her hair stayed sternly mid-Victorian in style, whether playing a dark ages Lady Macbeth or, as here, a scintillating Italian maiden. She was, however, an admirable foil to Kean, and the real leading spirit at the Princess's Theatre. She undertook the training of the young actors and actresses, among whom was the young Ellen Terry, who never forgot her debt to Mrs. Kean's severe but thorough training. *(SW)*

Charles Kean (1811–1868), English actor and manager, son of Edmund Kean, who first appeared on stage in 1827 and played Iago opposite his father's fatal last Othello in 1833. With his wife **Ellen Tree** (1806–1880), he rose to the head of his profession, notably through his management of the Princess's Theatre from 1851 to 1859.

Mr. and Mrs. Charles Kean as Benedick and Beatrice
in *Much Ado About Nothing*
Photograph by Laroche, **coloured by hand**
Guy Little Collection

We allude to Grimaldi, but must not indulge ourselves on the subject, or we should have no end in describing his tricks and devices, his grins and shoulder-shakings . . . his expressions of childish glee in gigglings and squeaks, his facile dislocation of limbs . . . , his short and deep snatches of laughter . . . in short, all those perfections of the clown which before his time perhaps were confined to the Italian stage.

LEIGH HUNT (**THE EXAMINER**, 12 FEBRUARY 1815)

When John Rich first anglicized pantomime in the early eighteenth century Harlequin was the dominant figure, but at the beginning of the nineteenth century a new comic genius arose who was to shift the accent of the Harlequinade, and to become the pantomime clown above all others. Acrobat, dancer, juggler, and actor, Joseph Grimaldi possessed the attributes of all performers of Clown, but in a higher degree. To audiences the Clown symbolized anarchy: he was irreverent, opposed to law and order, a liar, cheat, glutton, rogue, coward.

Within these common traits, Grimaldi developed his own type of 'transformation' or 'construction' scenes, two of which are featured opposite, and in which he revealed an almost childlike vision of the tangible world, a joy in turning prosaic objects into things of wonder by sheer force of the imagination. Thus, in the pantomime *The Red Dwarf* Grimaldi transformed himself into a Bold Dragoon – black coal scuttles became cavalry boots, real horseshoes shod the heels, brass dishes became the spurs, the pelisse was formed by a white bearskin, the cap was a muff, the tassel a table brush, while a black tippet provided him with a suitable beard, side whiskers and moustache. It hardly needed the presence of several real Hussars in the audience to make the point, and it was not surprising that Grimaldi's practical satire won him the title of 'Hogarth in action'.

One of the traditional functions of the Clown was, of course, to be the butt of the other characters, and Grimaldi's genius in the role did not save him from the traditional beatings given to the Clown by all the other pantomime characters in turn. The pantomime *Harlequin and Asmodeus* in 1810 was no exception. The ultimate degradation came when, again exercising a child's love of building something out of something else, Grimaldi built a man out of vegetables, only to be ignominiously beaten off the stage by the inhuman creature of his own creation. *(SW)*

Joseph Grimaldi (1778–1837), English pantomime clown, son of Giuseppe Grimaldi, ballet master at Drury Lane. He first appeared at Sadler's Wells Theatre when he was two years old, and as an adult played in the pantomime Harlequinades at Sadler's Wells, Covent Garden, Drury Lane, and on tour. From 1822 his health deteriorated, partly due to the physical risks he took in his extremely athletic performances, and he retired in 1828.

Mr GRIMALDI, as CLOWN

in the Popular Pantomime of *HARLEQUIN & ASMODEUS*, now Performing at the Theatre Royal Covent Garden. Setting to with a Grotesque Figure which he makes up of a series of Vegetables, Fruit &c. and which becoming Animated beats him off the Stage.

GRIMALDI, Bold Dragoon in the Popular Pantomime of the Red Dwarf

Joseph Grimaldi
i in *Harlequin and Asmodeus*
(Theatre Royal, Covent Garden, 1810) R. Norman
Published by R. Ackermann, 8 February 1811
Etching coloured by hand 245 × 325
Harry R. Beard Collection. f.62–35
ii as the Bold Dragoon in *The Red Dwarf*
(Theatre Royal, Covent Garden, 1812) Anonymous
Etching coloured by hand 244 × 350
Harry R. Beard Collection. f.67–33

> He [Lewis Casson] says I'm not the least bit suited to Hecuba – blast her – and I know it, so what does he want to rub it in for? . . . I loathe the way I play her more than he does, but I will play her one day, if it's only to say 'Sucks' to Lewis.

SYBIL THORNDIKE (IN RUSSELL THORNDIKE, **SYBIL THORNDIKE,** 1929)

With characteristic humility and dissatisfaction, Sybil Thorndike accepted the strictures of her husband and director Lewis Casson about her performance as Hecuba in Euripides's *The Trojan Women* at the Old Vic in 1919. When she began to study the role she felt that her voice lacked control, and that she did not look like the conventional tragic heroine. 'Mine is really a vicar's wife's face – it's tragic for me the way I want to do all things my face doesn't fit', she once wrote. In fact, her thrilling, vibrant voice had reached maturity and was perfectly attuned to the cadences of Gilbert Murray's translation, catching for her audience the 'inner meaning of living' that Lewis Casson regarded as the primary aim of the actor.

The photograph opposite catches the monumental qualities of her performance as Hecuba, mourning for Troy in its final hours, laments over the dead before the final voyage into slavery. This is not an individual suffering, it is a symbol of a nation, a symbol of all who are left to endure living with suffering. In 1919 Sybil Thorndike brought to her interpretation her own experiences of the First World War, her own fears for her husband in France, the tragic loss of her youngest brother Frank in 1917, and the subsequent death of her father. To this she added her maternal emotions (the child in her arms is her own son Christopher) and the burning conviction of her own pacifism.

While the critics were unanimous in their praise, the majority of the playgoing public, growing up amid a theatre of 'naturalism' and understatement, found it difficult to respond to playing of such tragic grandeur. It was typical of Sybil Thorndike that she felt her greatest tribute came from an old cockney woman who said: 'Well, dearie, me and me pals went to see your play, it was lovely, and we all 'ad a good cry and a nice walk home over the bridge and I got 'em some shrimps for tea. You see, them Trojans was just like us. We've lost our sons and 'usbands in this bleedin' war, 'aven't we? So no wonder we was all cryin'. That was a real play, that was, dearie.' *(SW)*

Sybil Thorndike (1882–1976), English actress, who made her stage début in 1904 and then toured with Ben Greet for three years in America. On her return in 1908 she married Lewis Casson and joined Miss Horniman's company at the Gaiety Theatre, Manchester. Her long career embraced both classical and modern plays notably *St. Joan* (1924), specially written for her by Shaw, Aase in Ibsen's *Peer Gynt* (1944), and Greek drama. She was created D.B.E. in 1931 and Companion of Honour in 1970.

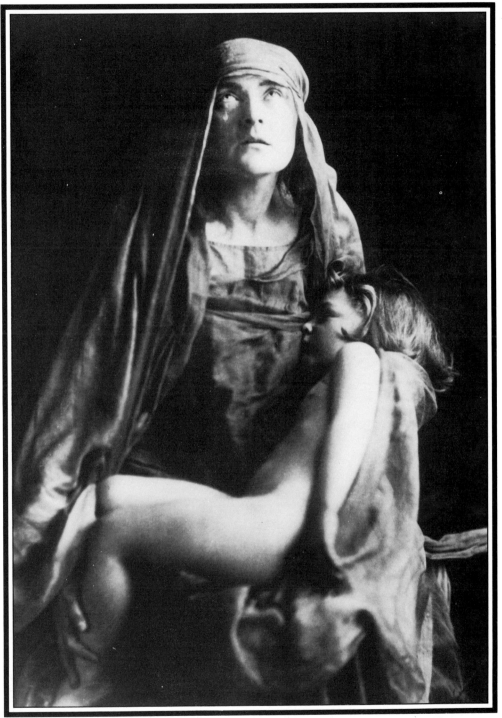

Sybil Thorndike as Hecuba in *The Trojan Women*, 1919
Photograph by Florence Vandamm

> The attitudes which we take have an influence upon our soul. A simple throwing back of the head, done passionately, causes us a sudden tremor of joy, of heroism, or of desire. All gestures have a moral resonance, and thus can directly express every possible moral state.
>
> ISADORA DUNCAN (QUOTED IN J. E. CRAWFORD FLITCH, **MODERN DANCING AND DANCERS**, 1912)

The beginning of the twentieth century saw a reaction against formal classical ballet, especially in America and Germany where there was no strong heritage of dance. Isadora Duncan was one of the first to cast aside the constricting contemporary dance dress, and perform barefoot in Greek-inspired draperies, dancing to the music of the great classical masters. As a rebel against all formal training, she left no specific influence on technique; her dances, though carefully prepared, had a strong improvisatory quality and so did not survive her death. Rather, she revealed the body's capacity to evoke emotion as potently as poetry or music.

She was a self-taught dancer, rejecting formal training, and scorning ballet as unnatural, rigid, and inexpressive. She wanted to express in movement, and from nature alone, the essence of life rather than specific character or situation. She did not directly translate music into movement, but rather used it as the springboard for an emotional impulse that could only find expression in dance. Most crucial for her personal style was the discovery that the centre of movement lay in the solar plexus –'the crater of motor power, the unity from which all diversities of movements are born . . . when I had learned to concentrate all my force to this one Centre I found that thereafter when I listened to music the rays and vibrations of the music streamed to this one fount of light within me'.

Isadora Duncan's impact upon European dance can be gauged from the many artists, including Rodin, who found inspiration in her work. José Clara's drawing gives an idea of her effect upon audiences. She was possessed by the intensity of feeling: hers was no charming, decorative entertainment, nor was she superficially feminine, but monumental, epic – the epitome of the mature woman, the 'earth mother' of Greek legend. Clara himself wrote after seeing her in 1902: 'When she appeared we all had the feeling that God – that is to say Certainty, Simplicity, Grandeur and Harmony – that God was present . . . the finest dreams and highest visions were born and unfolded through the magic of her movements'. *(SW)*

Isadora Duncan (1878–1927), self-taught American dancer, who, after her début in Chicago in 1899, toured Europe, establishing a school in Berlin in 1904, and in the following year making the first of many visits to Russia. She started her Moscow school in 1921, but her methods were impossible to convey, having no teachable technical foundation.

Isadora Duncan
José Clara
Editions Rieder, 1928
Collotype 327 × 251

I love the art of pantomime. I love to go through a scene and represent a character where there is neither singing nor speaking; only to feel and understand what I have to express, and carry it out by sheer acting, that is, with attitude, *geste*, glance of the eye, pointing of the hand or a finger.

ADELINA PATTI (QUOTED IN HERMAN KLEIN, **THE REIGN OF PATTI,** 1920)

Both Mario and Fauré were well-known singers of the roles of Faust and Mephistopheles at the time of the performance illustrated opposite. In Gounod's *Faust* Marguerite is seduced by Faust with the aid of Mephistopheles, incarnation of the devil. She loses her reason after the murder of her brother, and kills the son she had by Faust before dying herself, calling for divine mercy. In this photograph of the scene in the garden, Mephistopheles woos the neighbour Marthe while Faust declares his love to Marguerite.

Gounod himself had thought at Adelina Patti's Paris début that she would make the ideal Marguerite, and she first sang the role in Hamburg in 1863. In London, as *The Illustrated London News* pointed out, she had one great advantage over rivals in the role, 'the resistless charm derived from the delicious freshness of early youth'. It was Patti's London début at Covent Garden as Marguerite which led even Henry Chorley, one of her severest critics, to admit in *The Athenaeum*: 'Obviously, every note of the music, every word of the text, every change of the situation, had been thought over, and been felt by the artist'.

Patti's detractors criticized her preoccupation with the beauty of her voice rather than with what she was singing. She was fond of vocal embellishment, and Rossini declared after hearing her sing 'Una Voce' that he was unable to recognize his own music. She also dressed and acted as a true *prima donna*, always playing to her audience and taking countless curtain calls. In spite of this, she had a remarkably beautiful voice and genuine dramatic instinct. Her joy in her own singing was infectious and transferred itself to those who were fortunate enough to hear her. *(CEH)*

Adelina Patti (1843–1919), Italian soprano, who toured the USA as a child prodigy, made her European début at Covent Garden as Amina in Bellini's *La Somnambula* in 1861, and sang there regularly until her six 'farewell' performances in 1895. **Giovanni Mario** (1810–1883), Italian tenor, who made his London début as Gennaro in Donizetti's *Lucrezia Borgia* in 1839, created the title role in Costa's *Don Carlos* (1844), and from 1847 sang regularly at Covent Garden until his retirement in 1871. **Jean-Baptiste Fauré** (1830–1914), French baritone, who made his début in Massé's *Galathée* at the Opéra-Comique in 1852. He first appeared in London at Covent Garden in 1860, and created the role of Charles VII in Mermet's *Jeanne d'Arc* in Paris (1876).

Mario (right) as Faust, **Adelina Patti** as Marguerite,
and **Jean-Baptiste Fauré** as Mephistopheles in *Faust*
(Royal English Opera, Covent Garden, 1864)
Photograph by Caldesi and Co.
Guy Little Collection

> In order to taint and undermine the morals of our ingenuous youth, [the French] sent among us a number of female dancers, who by the allurements of the most indecent attitudes, and most wanton theatrical exhibitions, succeeded but too effectually in loosening and corrupting the moral feelings of the people.
>
> BISHOP SHUTE BARRINGTON OF DURHAM (TO THE HOUSE OF LORDS, 1798)

Pictured here are Charles Didelot, his wife Mme Rose, and Mlle Parisot, all French-trained dancers who frequently appeared in London in the late eighteenth century. Ballet in England at this time was not a full evening's entertainment, but restricted to *entr'actes* or short afterpieces performed in the same bill as operas or plays. *Alonzo e Cora* (altered by Gillray to *Alonzo e Caro*) was just such an afterpiece, first seen at the King's Theatre in London on 2 April 1796, based on *Les Incas* by Jean-François Marmontel – hence the image of the sun in the background of the print, the expression on its face reflecting contemporary disapproval of the scanty, diaphanous dresses worn by female dancers during the 1790s (Mlle Parisot especially seems to have favoured the minimum of costume, for she is invariably portrayed with one breast bare).

The French Revolution had ushered in an era of dress inspired by Graeco-Roman draperies, and dancers were quick to adopt the new costume. The adoption of flesh-coloured tights and the development of the heelless slipper also gave greater flexibility to the foot, and with the body thus able to move more freely there was an immediate increase in the range of steps that women could perform, including attitudes, jumps, and pirouettes. The way was now open for the development of the *pas de deux* – impossible when women had worn panniered skirts – and the development of *pointe* work.

Though a caricature, this etching by Gillray (1757–1815) does capture the grace and style of the dancers. Didelot and Mme Rose's performances in 1796 were highly praised, in contrast to Didelot's appearance in 1789, when the audience rioted because they felt he was not up to standard. *The True Briton* stated 'We never witnessed more genteel mobbing in our lives. . . . Didelot and Rose were the magnetic objects of curiosity . . . public expectation has seldom been more fully gratified'. Their *pas de deux* in *Alonzo e Cora* was hailed as 'the prettiest thing that year' and in the name of patriotism a special *pas de trois* danced to 'God Save the King' was inserted. *(SW)*

Charles-Louis Didelot (1767–1837), French dancer, choreographer, and teacher who made his début in London in 1788, and later choreographed his most famous ballet, *Flore et Zéphyre*, for the King's Theatre in 1796. From 1801 to 1811 and from 1816 he was ballet master in St. Petersburg, reorganizing the system of teaching and laying foundations for the later St. Petersburg style. His wife, **Rose Pole**, died in St. Petersburg in 1803. Among his ballets were *Apollo and Daphne* (1802), *Cupid and Psyche* (1810), *The Prisoner of the Caucasus* (1823), and the first Russian production of Dauberval's *La Fille mal gardée*.

Charles Didelot with his wife **Mme Rose** (left) and
Mlle Parisot in *Alonzo e Cora*
(King's Theatre, London, 1796)
James Gillray
Published by H. Humphrey, 5 May 1796
Etching coloured by hand 257 × 357
Harry R. Beard Theatre Collection. f.120–23

[*Othello*] was done Elizabethan, and I don't think Paul Robeson's costume was right for him. Negroes tend to bend their knees as they walk, and his dress demanded straight knees. In his white robe at the end he looked superb, and Peggy was so lovely and so gallant. I wish we had voices in the theatre like his now – deep, vibrant, masculine notes. We really seem to lack bass speaking voices today.

SYBIL THORNDIKE (QUOTED IN ELIZABETH SPRIGGE, **SYBIL THORNDIKE**, 1971)

Othello was Paul Robeson's first attempt at playing classical drama, and he became the first American negro to play the role in London since Ira Aldridge over sixty years before. He chose as his Desdemona a promising young actress, Peggy Ashcroft, while Sybil Thorndike was engaged as Emilia, and Maurice Browne (who also managed the production) played Iago.

The painter James Pryde was engaged to design the scenery, his first work for the theatre. The sets were massively impressive but built far upstage, which, as James Agate caustically remarked, gave the impression that the actors were all performing in the next room. To maintain the effect of Pryde's painting they were also rather dimly lit, so that Robeson's face all but disappeared at times, and rumour had it that Ralph Richardson concealed a torch in his sleeve to find his way about. Illusion was not helped by the weight of the sets which were impossible to move quietly. The bed, as the cartoon of Haselden (1872–1953) suggests, was 'fourteen feet high and timbered like a schooner' (Eric Keown): the noise of it being trundled into position effectively drowned Peggy Ashcroft's 'willow' song.

In the event Ashcroft was the success of the evening. John Gielgud, who saw her for the first time on the production's first night, recalled that when she first came on in the Senate scene wearing a gold dress 'it was as if the sun had come out'. Robeson himself was hampered by Elizabethan dress, and despite the beauty of his voice he was not experienced in speaking blank verse. Not until he appeared in the final scene, wearing a white kaftan, did he look truly impressive. Agate, however, recalled the touching simplicity of his meeting with Desdemona, and the magnificent power of the third and fourth acts 'rendered with magnificent power, so that Othello ceased to be human and became a gibbering primeval man', while 'the last act achieved dignity and pathos'.

(SW)

Paul Robeson (1898–1976), American negro actor and singer, who made his stage début in New York, 1921, and in London as Brutus Jones in *The Emperor Jones* in 1925. While best known as a concert singer, his stage roles included 'Yank' in O'Neill's *The Hairy Ape* (1931), Joe in *Showboat* (1928), and Othello in the 1943 New York production.

Peggy Ashcroft (b. 1907), English actress, who made her début at Birmingham Rep in 1926 in Barrie's *Dear Brutus*. She became famous after playing Juliet in Gielgud's production of *Romeo and Juliet* in 1935, and was later acclaimed in a wide range of roles from Shakespeare (Beatrice, Mistress Page, Queen Margaret) to Chekhov, Ibsen (Hedda Gabler), and Beckett. Created D.B.E. in 1956, she became a director of the Royal Shakespeare Company in 1968.

Desdemona ... Miss Peggy Ashcroft
Othello ..... Mr. Paul Robeson

"Othello" (Savoy)
Punch: 28 May 1930

Peggy Ashcroft as Desdemona and **Paul Robeson** as
Othello (Savoy Theatre, London, 1930)
W. K. Haselden
Original artwork for *Punch*, 28 May 1930
Pen and ink 273 × 184
Gabrielle Enthoven Collection

> Musically and creatively, I have always been an instigator rather than an artisan. I want to retain the position of being a photostat machine with an image, because I think that most songwriters are anyway.
>
> DAVID BOWIE (QUOTED IN **BOWIE – LIVES AND TIMES**)

Photographed in grim Earl's Court, this Bowie of the industrial age, in monochrome costume under harsh neon lighting, imbued with pessimism and disillusion, is one of the later 'photostats'. It is a long way from the *persona* of the early part of his career – a wavy-haired acoustic hippy singing his odd little 'Space Oddity'. In 1969, in the wave of heavy metal and skinheads that despatched the remnants of flower-power to the compost heap, this style was totally incongruous and constant harassment forced Bowie off the dance-hall circuit.

Musically, his interests turned to the half-world of insanity, bisexual loneliness, and alienation. Partially drawing on his work with the mime Lindsay Kemp, Bowie's next incarnation was his androgynous *alter ego* Ziggy Stardust, interplanetary tart and Messiah of the Apocalypse. With orange-spiked hair, zigzag make-up, and rhinestone-encrusted leotard, Ziggy spawned thousands of adoring clones who misused their mums' lipsticks and created glam-rock, but when audiences started calling for 'Ziggy' and not 'David' Bowie killed off Stardust and announced his retirement in July 1973.

Throughout the 1970s new faces of Bowie appeared: Aryan race-hero, New York *chic-élite*, sybaritic darling of the 1930s – not to mention flirtations with German Expressionism and 'industrial music'. It has been argued that this constant theatricality tends to overshadow and undermine Bowie as a performer and songwriter, but in some ways his main contribution to rock is his talent in creating theatre and successfully marketing the product.

Pennie Smith here catches Bowie as the actor rather than the singer, divorced from the microphone, communicating through eyes, hands, and body, as well as voice. The photography concentrates on the image and hardly attempts to convey music, a technique that reinforces Bowie's self-awareness in performance. He is conscious that he is a commodity and has spoken of the need for 'unabashed prostitution' in rock: by exulting in the fact that he prostitutes his art and soul on vinyl and in performance, he shows greater integrity than those who do the same but refuse to comment on their traffic with such commerce. *(DF)*

David Bowie [Jones] (b. 1947), English writer, instrumentalist, vocalist, actor, producer, and arranger, who ran his own groups before working with Lindsay Kemp's Mime Troupe in 1967–68. After 'Space Oddity' (1969) he directed Beckenham Arts Laboratory, making the albums 'The Man Who Sold the World' (1970) and 'Hunky Dory' (1971) before producing his smash hit 'The Rise and Fall of Ziggy Stardust and the Spiders from Mars' (1972). In the USA he recorded 'Young Americans' (1975) and acted in the film 'The Man Who Fell to Earth' (released 1976). In 1980 he acted the title role of *The Elephant Man* on Broadway, toured the USA, and brought out 'Scary Monsters and Super Creeps'.

David Bowie performing (Earl's Court, London, 1978)
Photograph by Pennie Smith

> We did not at first understand a word; we did not understand his walk; nor any of his movements; but he gripped us, he interested us, he excited us, and the excitement increased and increased, until, when the last curtain fell, we could only sit, gasping, stunned and silent.
>
> ACCOUNT OF IRVING IN **THE BELLS** (QUOTED IN R. FINDLATER, **THE PLAYER KINGS,** 1971)

All actor-managers had one role in their repertoire with which they were particularly identified: Henry Irving's was Mathias in *The Bells*, first created in 1871. The character of Mathias as conceived by Irving hardly exists in the original Leopold Lewis melodrama, where action, not character, is paramount. An innkeeper is haunted by the memory of a murder he committed many years before, symbolized in his mind by the sound of sleigh-bells associated with the victim. In his imagination he is tried and condemned, and the play ends with his self-induced death from guilt and fear.

Irving totally immersed himself in the character of Mathias. His facial expressions were 'an index of his mind, changeful, capricious, now sunny with smiles, now gloomy with impending storm ... [not] a mere trick of affectation of art, but the natural changes in the countenance that denote agony or relief to the tortured mind' (Clement Scott). The photographs opposite have frozen the flow of emotion into isolated instants through which one can grasp something of Irving's hypnotic power: the famous moment when, bending to fasten his shoe, Mathias hears someone refer to the old murder, and the guilty wariness as the body stiffens in temporary fear; the terror as he imagines he hears the jangling bells.

Playing of this intensity was an immense strain, and Irving could never act Mathias with ease. As Ellen Terry recalled: 'Every time he heard the sound of the bells, the throbbing of his heart must have nearly killed him. He used always to turn quite white – there was no trick to it. It was imagination acting physically on the body. His death as Mathias – the death of a strong, robust man – was different from all his other stage deaths. He did really almost die – he imagined death with such horrible intensity. His eyes would disappear upwards, his face grow grey, his limbs cold.' In 1905 a doctor warned him never to play the role again as the strain on his heart would be too great. Irving disregarded this advice, and 'within twenty-four hours of his last death as Mathias, he was dead' (Ellen Terry). *(SW)*

Henry Irving [John Henry Brodribb] (1838–1905), English actor-manager, who made his professional début in 1856 and his first London appearance in 1866. He managed the Lyceum Theatre from 1878, and was renowned for meticulous productions and performances both of Shakespeare and of Victorian plays, including Boucicault's *The Corsican Brothers* (1880), Wills's *Faust* (1885), and Tennyson's *Becket* (1893). He toured the USA and Canada extensively, and last appeared at the Lyceum in 1902. His success did much to make the stage respectable and he was the first actor to be knighted in 1895.

Henry Irving as Mathias in *The Bells*, c. 1871
Carte-de-visite photographs by London
Stereoscopic Co.
Guy Little Collection

The programme for the Alhambra revue *Everything New? Not Likely* carried the credits below for the scene illustrated opposite. They are couched in the pun-ridden form of mid-Victorian pantomime, which by the end of the nineteenth century had become a subject for burlesque in its own right. The Alhambra *Robinson Crusoe* is a parody of a burlesque, for, where the burlesque retained the tradition of the Principal Boy being played by a girl (see No. 58), here the role is taken by a man costumed as the Principal Boy. *(SW)*

"ROBINSON CRUSOE"

OR

" The Diabolical Davy Jones, whose dastardly deeds are frustrated by the Fearless Fairy, who waves her witching wand and rescues Peter Pan Robinson from his perilous predicament."

A GORGEOUS AND SPECTACULAR PANTOMIME IN SIX SPASMS AND OCCASIONAL INTERLUDES, BY ROBERT HALE.

The Plot was hatched at HATCHETT'S.

(Anyone daring to infringe the copyright of this story will receive an Iron Cross.

Music stolen by GELVILLE MIDEON.—Lyrics forged by SWEARS.—Costumes designed by MacST.—Tights by TAUTZ.—Shoes by SHOOLBRED. Dances and Ensembles by MAPLE.   Stage Production by HANDBILL LARKER.

The Names of others responsible for the Production excised by The Censor.

NOTE.—The Doctor is always in attendance. Morphia may be obtained at the Bars.

The Demon King (A naughty gnome who stops at naught)	Mr. Lynch	Polly (Robin's sweetheart, Principal Girl)	Miss MONKMAN	
Good Fairy Cockleshell (who never goes to Night Clubs)	Miss de Bausche	Captain Capstan (The captivating Commander, 2nd Principal Boy) ..	Miss Mercer	
		Louisa (His girl, 2nd Principal Girl)	Miss Wollaston	
Seaweed / Good little Fairies specially engaged for this production from the A.B.C. Co.	Miss Hope	Violet (3rd Principal Boy)	Miss Graham	
Golden Sand	Miss Rossiter	Beryl (3rd Principal Girl)	Miss Gwynne	
Silver Fin	Miss Oliver	Nellie (4th Principal Boy)	Miss Jarman	
Star Fish	Miss Daly	Violet (4th Principal Girl)	Miss Ashton	
		Madge (5th Principal Boy)	Miss Thorpe	
Will Atkins (The Wicked Pirate King)	Mr. MORRISON	Rosa (5th Principal Girl)	Miss Sullivan	
		Cannibal King	Mr. Sims	
Billy Crusoe (Robin's saucy brother)	Mr. Leslie	Friday	Mr. Stuart	
		The Goat	Mr. Kaufmann	
Mrs. Crusoe (Robin's Mother)	Mr. Desmond	The Monkey	Mr. Nagle	
		The Parrot	Miss Barrett	
		The Lightening King ..	Mr. Desmond	
ROBINSON CRUSOE		Mr. ROBERT HALE		

Scene I. . . . **" Davy Jones's Locker under the Thames."**

(WILLINGS)

The Costumes in this Scene by BOOTS CASH CHEMISTS.
Goblets, Ignomes and Spirits by TOMMY DEWAR.   The Good Fairy's Wand by SELFRIDGE.
The Demon's Cauldron lighted by THE GAS LIGHT & COKE CO.
OYSTERS in the River bed by HARRY HEM.

Scene II. . . . . **" Mill Wall Docks."**

(WILL CROOKS)

The Boat used in this Scene kindly lent by THE WHITE STAR LINE.
Polly's Costume by TRUE-FIT.   Robin's Costume by MISS-FITT.
Mrs. Crusoe's Laundry by THE GARDEN CITY CO.

Scene III. . . . . . **" Between Decks."**

Scene IV. . . . . . **" The Pirate Ship."**

Thunder and Lightening supplied by GEORGE BERNHARDI SHAW.
The Mast and Rigging supervised by TOMMY LIPTON.

This Scene will be followed by a realistic and thrilling Storm, in which the good ship sinks.

Scene V. . . . . . **" The Raft. Saved!"**

Scene VI. . . . . . **" The Cannibal Island."**

This Island was especially discovered for this Production by THEODORE ROOSEVELT.
Friday's Fire supplied by the SAVOY GRILL.
Savages kindly lent by the SAVAGE CLUB.   Engaged through Blackamore Agency.
Animals kindly lent by C. B. COCHRAN from the WONDER ZOO, and trained by ATTY-PERSEE.

Robert Hale as Robinson Crusoe rescuing Man Friday
(**Mr. Stuart**), while the Cannibal King (**Mr. Sims**) plots
in *Robinson Crusoe*, from *Everything New? Not Likely*
(Alhambra Theatre, London, 1914–15)
Photograph by Wrather and Buys
Gabrielle Enthoven Collection

When I went to Sadler's Wells I didn't have any special hopes. If I was going to get into the *corps de ballet* and be in the back row or do some small solos or character dances I should have been quite happy. Because I liked dancing and I didn't really think that I would ever get very far.

MARGOT FONTEYN IN INTERVIEW WITH RICHARD BUCKLE, 1964

Ondine, the nymph who forsakes her native element, the sea, to marry a mortal was one of Margot Fonteyn's greatest roles. She found the key to the character in the conflict between Ondine's unfettered nature and the human emotions she comes to experience, thus turning what could have been a charming trifle into great interpretive art. Cyril Beaumont recalled 'her pale, intensely expressive features framing her dark trailing hair like floating sea-grass, her spume-coloured dress spotted with dew . . . she creates the illusion of a being from another sphere, infinitely curious about the strange world of mortals – guileless, childlike, wayward, and capricious, yet elusive and mysterious.'

The choreography reflected the very essence of water, with movements ranging from a bold sweeping use of the body (as in the photograph), suggesting a broad flowing river, to soft undulations of the arms, like a rippling mountain stream. Such fluidity of movement was an integral part of Fonteyn's individual dance style, which subordinated everything to the total effect and achieved perfect bodily harmony and an ideal marriage between dancing and acting.

The role of Ondine, first performed by Fonteyn at the Royal Opera House, Covent Garden on 27 October 1958, was created for her by the great English choreographer, Frederick Ashton, whose ballets not only laid the foundations of the Royal Ballet repertoire, but of the characteristic dance style of the company. A choreographer does not present his dancers with a finished script, since his raw material is the human body, moulded in rehearsal, and the resulting ballet is, therefore, influenced by the dancers available and their individual potential and their limitations. In Fonteyn, Ashton found the perfect qualities and temperament to give substance to his particular choreographic vision. In this, the last full-length ballet he made for her, Ashton gave Fonteyn the greatest gift a choreographer can bestow, a role that captured her qualities so perfectly that future generations seeing the ballet will be able to discern why Fonteyn was considered supreme among dancers of her generation. *(SW)*

Margot Fonteyn [Margaret Hookham] (b. 1919), English dancer, who joined the Vic-Wells (now Royal) Ballet in 1934. After the retirement of Alicia Markova in 1935 she became the company's ballerina, leaving in 1959 to further an independent international career. The first British ballerina of international stature, she became renowned for her interpretation of such classical roles as Princess Aurora in *The Sleeping Beauty* and Odette/Odile in *Swan Lake*. She was the inspiration for a host of roles choreographed by Frederick Ashton including Woman in Balldress in *Apparitions* (1936), *Symphonic Variations* (1946), Chloë in *Daphnis and Chloë* (1951), and Marguerite in *Marguerite and Armand* (1963). Created D.B.E. in 1956.

Margot Fonteyn in the title role of *Ondine*
(Royal Opera House, Covent Garden, *c.* 1958)
Photograph by Houston Rogers
Houston Rogers Collection

It was a November night, not inappropriately, of dense fog, and I recall it came right into the house, and I could hardly find my way round the stage. The fog went right into my throat, and I seem to remember it did something to my voice so that I couldn't sing the second night.

PETER PEARS RECALLING IN 1972 THE OPENING NIGHT OF **PETER GRIMES** AT COVENT GARDEN

Peter *Grimes* was Britten's first opera with immediate appeal, and is now an acknowledged masterpiece with a lasting place in the international repertoire. The story of *Peter Grimes*, with its anti-hero, is based on George Crabbe's poem 'The Borough' (1810). The opera opens in the moot hall of the Borough, an East Anglian fishing town, where an inquest is taking place which results in a verdict of accidental death for Grimes's apprentice boy. Ellen Orford, the schoolmistress, alone seems to believe in the innocence of Grimes, and later offers to fetch a replacement from the workhouse. Grimes overworks the boy, and Ellen quarrels with him. The men of the town decide to investigate, and Grimes leaves his hut with the boy, who accidentally falls to his death. Grimes puts his boat out to sea and sinks it.

In 1947 Joan Cross and Peter Pears were repeating the roles which they had sung in the premiere two years previously at Sadler's Wells. Many of the cast were dubious about the opera because the idiom was then so modern, but Joan Cross had few doubts: 'it had never occurred to me really and truly that we should have done anything else. Of course it was a huge success. It had a tremendous impact.'

Both Joan Cross and Peter Pears had strong links with Benjamin Britten. She left Sadler's Wells after disagreements with her fellow managers in 1945 to join Britten's English Opera Group, while the long and close association of Pears and Britten, from 1937 till Britten's death in 1976, resulted in a 'composer-interpreter relationship quite unique in musical history', and Britten wrote many of his works with the voice of Pears in mind. *(CEH)*

Joan Cross (b. 1900), English soprano and director. Principal soprano with Sadler's Wells Opera from 1931 to 1946, she became best known for her creation of several Britten roles: Ellen Orford in *Peter Grimes* (1945), Lady Billows in *Albert Herring* (Glyndebourne, 1947), and Elizabeth I in *Gloriana* (Covent Garden, 1953). A founder member of the English Opera Group, she was made a C.B.E. in 1951. **Peter Pears** (b. 1910), English tenor, best known for his life-long association from 1936 onwards with the composer Benjamin Britten, for whom he created many roles, from the Male Chorus in *The Rape of Lucretia* (1946) to Aschenbach in *Death in Venice* (1973). One of the founder members of the English Opera Group, he is still a director of the Aldeburgh Festival which he co-founded with Britten in 1948. Knighted in 1977.

Peter Pears in the title role and **Joan Cross** as Ellen
Orford in *Peter Grimes* (Royal Opera House, Covent
Garden, 1947)
Photograph by Angus McBean

The artists pictured here are just two acts out of the thousands working at the turn of the century when music hall had come to embrace a wide range of performers. Besides vocalists and comedians there were short dramatic scenes and ballets, jugglers, acrobats, magicians, illusionists, small animal acts, and novelty acts of many kinds.

The Kaufmann Troupe of Trick Bicyclists were also billed as Kaufmann's Lady Troupe or Cycling Beauties: 'The greatest and most Refined Cycle Act ever produced', trumpeted their publicity. They made their début at the Alhambra, one of London's leading music halls, in 1899, in an eight-week engagement at £40 a week, and seem to have been well received for they reappear from time to time on the Alhambra bills until Kaufmann broke up the act in 1912. The popularity of bicycling as a sport is reflected in the number of such cycling acts in music-hall programmes of this time, yet bicycles had been used in circus and music-hall acts as early as 1878. Six girls are pictured here, but the act could include as many as twelve, and it is obvious that the appeal of their act lay not least in its display of shapely figures at a time when fashions were concealing and constricting.

Negro performers began to appear in British theatres in the years following the American Civil War. (Minstrel groups, such as the Kentucky Minstrels and the Christy Minstrels, had flourished during the 1850s and 1860s, but the performers were white actors performing in black-face.) Many later famous names served their apprenticeships in minstrelsy in the 1880s and 1890s, and by this time, negro performers were becoming familiar in England. The musical novelty act illustrated opposite, the Six Musical Spillers, featured the saxophone, which had been patented by its Belgian inventor, Adolphe Sax, in 1846, but was still enough of a novelty for English audiences at the turn of the century for an act such as this to seek an engagement at one of London's major music halls. This photograph was among those sent by theatrical agents to Alfred Moul, the managing director of the Alhambra – one of thousands of such photographs he received annually from aspiring hopefuls. As far as can be ascertained, the Six Musical Spillers were among the large proportion of unsuccessful aspirants. *(SW)*

The Kaufmann Cycling Beauties and **Six Musical Spillers**
Early twentieth-century variety acts
Photographs by Ernst Schneider, and Apeda
Alfred Moul Collection

The difficulty about mastering circus time – when to pull yourself higher in a somersault or break out, to pirouette, to leave a flying bar . . . is the fact that there are no rules, no guidebooks, and no precision instruments by which to learn . . . there is nothing for the performer save a finely-developed sixth sense, which can neither be explained nor passed on. You simply learn when to let go, and until that finesse is developed, the most agile, most muscularly active person in the world is a failure as a performer.

ALFREDO CODONA (FROM 'SPLIT SECONDS', 1930, REPRINTED IN **THE CIRCUS: LURE AND LEGEND,** EDITED BY M.S. AND W. FENNER, 1970)

This aerial act is performed on a fixed cradle, a frame formed by two super-imposed bars about eighteen inches apart, and was part of a 'combined aerial sensation' comprising a Dutchman, 'Cubanos'; a Swede, Eric Soeder (and partner); and a Danish team, 'The Two Chalis' (Karl and Elsie Funk), who are probably the ones featured here. The bearer hangs head down from the bars, her knees over the first, and insteps under the second. Thus braced, she supports her partner from a pivot held between her teeth: he is hanging by one arm and, once balanced, will begin spinning.

In another part of their act she was again the bearer, this time holding in her hands two ropes, each ending in a ring, on which her partner performed the balancing act. Another variation performed in the combined act involved the man as bearer, holding in one hand a pole from the end of which his partner, suspended horizontally in the air, hung by her teeth.

In contrast to a flying trapeze act, which stresses ease and grace, this act, performed high above the circus ring, is a test of strength and endurance. On a hot day, the combination of the heat of the lights and the rising heat from a massed audience creates a stifling atmosphere in the dome of the Big Top and temperatures of 132 degrees Fahrenheit have been recorded. An audience, aware of the obvious dangers of the aerial acts, is, however, usually unaware of this additional hazard. *(SW)*

Aerial act, Bertram Mills' Circus
(Olympia, London, 1948–49)
Photograph by Baron Nicholas de Rakoczy

In no other part that I have played have I found it so difficult to know whether I became Hamlet or Hamlet became me, for the association of an actor with such a character is an extraordinarily subtle transformation, an almost indefinable mixture of imagination and impersonation.

JOHN GIELGUD (**STAGE DIRECTIONS**, 1963)

By 1944 John Gielgud had played Hamlet in four productions in fifteen years. His interpretation had obviously matured since he first played the role at the Old Vic in 1930, when he was 26: Hamlet was now a man rather than an impulsive, intense young Prince, and the actor was re-creating youth and its emotions rather than experiencing them directly.

Born into the Terry family, Gielgud has always been aware of himself as part of a continuing theatrical tradition, and when he went to the Old Vic in 1929 to learn to play Shakespeare he was making a conscious bid to claim the 'noble inheritance' of the great classical roles. He had already seen ten or twelve actors play Hamlet, and this created a particular problem: 'My mind has been torn in studying the part between a desire to walk in the tradition of the great ones and to carve out some interpretation that I might justly call my own'. Because rehearsal time was limited, he threw himself directly into the role and found that 'it would hold me up if I sought the truth in it'. He let the flow of the verse guide him towards the final interpretation and slowly realized that the words were finding an emotional echo in his own experience.

At 26, Gielgud was one of the youngest actors to play Hamlet since the fourteen-year-old Master Betty over a century before, and his age alone was enough to throw new light on the familiar situations, his youthful hysteria and uncertainty helping to make Hamlet's dilemma understandable. Gielgud was well aware that Hamlet is the greatest 'juvenile lead' of all, and the photograph opposite captures the noble romanticism and youthful vulnerability that he brought to the role. Victorian actors had often thought Hamlet's attack on Gertrude distasteful, but Gielgud found that showing an unsympathetic side of his nature helped to round out Hamlet's character. For Gielgud, the performance was a turning point in his development as an actor: 'I tried to seek for what was true in myself, for the first time, I think, both good and bad, so that the balance was a true person'. *(SW)*

John Gielgud (b. 1904), English actor, who made his stage début at the Old Vic in 1921, then established himself in the West End taking over as Nicky in Coward's *The Vortex* in 1925 and Lewis Dodd in *The Constant Nymph* (1926). Returning to the Old Vic in 1929 to play Shakespearian leads, he was acclaimed for his Hamlet and Richard II, and as a distinguished interpreter of a wide range of roles including Chekhov and Wilde. As manager of the Queen's Theatre, 1937–38, and again at the Haymarket Theatre, 1944–45, he attempted to establish a repertory company in the West End. In more recent years he has appeared in modern plays by Alan Bennett, Edward Bond, Charles Wood, and Harold Pinter. Knighted in 1953. **Martita Hunt** (1900–1969), English actress who made her début in 1921, and established her reputation playing the Governess in Chekhov's *The Cherry Orchard* (1926) before taking Shakespearian leads opposite Gielgud at the Old Vic, 1929–30. Well-known as Miss Havisham in Dickens's *Great Expectations* (1939), and for her many film roles.

John Gielgud as Hamlet with **Martita Hunt** as
Gertrude (Old Vic, London, 1930)
Photograph by J. W. Debenham
British Theatre Museum Association

She was always to me 'Our Lady of Sighs'– of a beautiful sadness in no way akin to the doleful dumps of Duse or the tragic splendour of Sarah – the sadness that is in the eyes of Botticelli's angels.

W. GRAHAM ROBERTSON (**LETTERS FROM GRAHAM ROBERTSON,**
EDITED BY KERRISON PRESTON, 1953)

In 1882 Ellen Terry was entering her great years as an actress, and Juliet was to be her most important role since she had become Henry Irving's leading lady at the Lyceum in 1878. *Romeo and Juliet* was planned as the most elaborate of all Lyceum productions, a series of breathtaking stage pictures that, in the event, smothered the play and made it difficult to concentrate on the acting. Juliet's balcony was thus 'a marble terrace of an ancient palace, underneath the roof supported by solid pillars. Around this cool and overhanging temple, as it seemed, grew the richest foliage – real trees, most of them growing in a deep umbrageous ravine, through which the moon shone cold and clear' (Clement Scott).

It was perhaps this effect that the photographers, Window and Grove, tried to re-create in their studio when Ellen Terry went to them for one of her frequent photo sessions. Their photograph captures the qualities that observers noted in her balcony scene: no artifice or coquetry, but grace, serenity, and complete naturalness. There is also a hint of wistful sadness, that, according to Graham Robertson, infused her roles during her greatest years. 'Her eyes were always infinitely sad. Perhaps that was why she succeeded so wonderfully in scenes of too great happiness – happiness that was "fey" and must forebode sorrow'.

Her Juliet was generally felt to be lacking in fire and depth, and Ellen Terry herself was not pleased with her performance. She had studied extensively, reading commentaries on the character and accounts of what other actresses had done in the role. But in retrospect she felt she should have gone direct to Verona and soaked up its atmosphere, or relied solely on the play and allowed her own instinct (usually infallible) to guide her towards an interpretation.

Irving admired the performance, however, even rating it above her much-acclaimed Portia, and Sarah Bernhardt was impressed particularly by the fact that Ellen could weep real tears on stage night after night. As Mrs. Patrick Campbell acidly remarked about Ellen's illustrious great-nephew: 'The Terrys always cry so easily'. *(SW)*

Ellen Terry (1847–1928), English actress, who made her début aged nine as Mamillius in Charles Kean's production of *The Winter's Tale* (1856). As Henry Irving's leading lady at the Lyceum from 1878 to 1896, she played Shakespeare's heroines as well as leads in Victorian plays such as *The Lady of Lyons, Becket*, and *Charles I*. Her later roles included those in Barrie's *Alice-Sit-By-The-Fire* and in Shaw's *Captain Brassbound's Conversion*, both specially written for her. She was created a D.B.E. in 1925.

Ellen Terry as Juliet
Photograph by Window and Grove
Guy Little Collection

I think of her in terms of basic gesture. I think of her age, her class – very important for the hands – her period, and her fate. There are two or three gestures that are essential to that character and indissoluble from her.

MARIA CALLAS ON REHEARSING A ROLE (IN IDA COOK, **WE FOLLOWED OUR STARS,** 1976)

Whenever Maria Callas performed she aroused controversy. Her vocal technique was sometimes imperfect, but the dramatic intensity she brought to her roles was admired even by her sternest critics. Martin Cooper said of Cherubini's *Medea* that it was 'an opera of great expectations aroused but not always fully realized'. But Callas injected into the role a great dramatic interpretation which the music could not fully support: 'the sheer intensity of Callas's conception unbalances the whole'.

In Act III, illustrated opposite, Medea kills her two children and sets fire to the temple. Jason, the father of her children, has betrayed them by marrying Glauce, to whom she has sent a poisoned diadem and cloak as wedding gifts. For Medea, life has ended and revenge is all that is left: killing her children takes them away from a life of betrayal. *Medea* was revived from obscurity as a vehicle for Callas by the Maggio Musicale Fiorentino in 1953. This was so successful that it was followed by other productions in Florence, Venice, Rome, and Dallas, all with Callas in the title role.

It is difficult, reading about Callas now, to discover exactly where the truth about her lies. The press seized upon all aspects of her personal and professional life. Disagreements with the managements of La Scala and the Metropolitan were blown up out of all proportion, as was her relationship with Onassis. But what is important about her is her contribution to the art of opera. We owe to her the revival of many *bel canto* roles, and a new realization of a high standard of dramatic interpretation.

Fortunately, she left many recordings behind her to support Harold Rosenthal's judgement: 'what was so remarkable was the use to which she put her by no means perfect vocal material, through sheer musical intelligence; and above all there was a quality inherent in her voice capable of moving the listener to tears'. *(CEH)*

Maria Callas (1923–1977), Greek soprano, born in New York, who studied at the Athens Conservatory with Elvira de Hidalgo. Her early heavy dramatic roles gave way to the *coloratura* range which realized her greatest potential, and the turning-point in her career came after she appeared under the conductor Tullio Serafin in 1947. She retired from opera as Tosca at Covent Garden in 1965, though she continued to give master classes and made an extensive concert tour in 1973 and 1974 with Giuseppe di Stefano.

Maria Callas in *Medea* (Royal Opera House, Covent Garden, 1959)
Photograph by Houston Rogers
Houston Rogers Collection

Deux Artistes Ingéneux
Dont les talents divers offrent l'accord Heureux
De la Grace unie à la force.

FROM THE LETTERING ON THE AQUATINT BASED ON THE SKETCH OPPOSITE

Up to the beginning of the nineteenth century, choreographers frequently turned to classical myths and legends to provide plots for ballets, and the story of Achilles's early life had been a favourite for many years before James Harvey D'Egville made a ballet on the subject in 1804. It was foretold of Achilles that he would either live a short and glorious life or a long and undistinguished one, so, hoping to keep him from danger, his mother Thetis disguised him as a girl and took him to live as handmaiden of the Princess Déidamie.

It was Ulysses who discovered the hiding-place, by a trick making Achilles reveal his true self, and together they embarked for the Trojan War. For a ballet, the story had the advantage of providing two contrasting male roles, in this case Achilles and Chiron (the centaur who teaches Achilles manly skills), in an age when the male dancers were still the star attractions in ballet.

James Harvey D'Egville was ballet-master at the King's Theatre in London between 1799 and 1809. He created his three-act ballet, *Achille et Déidamie* in 1804, one of its highlights being the extremely acrobatic *pas de deux* for himself as Chiron and Deshayes as Achilles. This occurred in the second act before Achilles leaves Chiron's cave and goes into disguise, according to the synopsis of the ballet published in *The True Briton* (1 February 1804). *Pas de deux* work in ballet was in its infancy, as the heavy formal costumes of the eighteenth century had precluded almost all close contact between dancers, and lifts such as shown in the drawing were almost unknown outside the work of tumblers and acrobats.

The *pas de deux* evidently aroused enough interest to warrant the publication of an aquatint a few months after the ballet was first performed on 31 January 1804. The drawing, probably by Jean Francois Huët-Villiers (1772–1813), reproduced here, appears to be a preliminary sketch for his better-known aquatint, and catches the muscular tension as Chiron supports Achilles. The actual sense of performance conveyed by the sketch is diminished to some extent in the aquatint, which opts for a more heroic approach and depicts Achilles as a larger and more dominant figure. *(SW)*

André Jean-Jacques Deshayes (1777–1846), French dancer and choreographer, who worked at the Paris Opéra and in Madrid and Milan before arriving in London at the King's Theatre, working there and at Her Majesty's Theatre until 1842. **James Harvey D'Egville** (c. 1770–c. 1836), English dancer and choreographer, who appeared in 1783 at the King's Theatre, and in the 1790s collaborated closely with Noverre, becoming choreographer at the King's from 1799 to 1809, composing music as well as choreographing ballets.

James Harvey D'Egville and **André Deshayes** in
Achille et Déidamie (King's Theatre, London, 1804)
Probably by J. F. M. Huët-Villiers
Pen and ink over pencil 216 × 145
Gabrielle Enthoven Collection, given by
L. E. Berman, Esq.

This passing of almost the last Great Romantic Figure of the past century seems to emphasize the death of Art and Beauty and to reveal the full dreariness of the ugly desert stretched around us. She was above all a high priestess of Beauty and would make any sacrifices for it.

W. GRAHAM ROBERTSON (**LETTERS FROM GRAHAM ROBERTSON**, EDITED BY KERRISON PRESTON, 1953)

By 1890 the 'Divine Sarah' was France's most celebrated actress, and, if her publicity is to be believed, it was her life's ambition to play Cleopatra. The play in which she did so, commissioned from Victorien Sardou and given its premiere at the Théâtre de la Porte-St-Martin in 1890, was no great literary masterpiece, but Bernhardt's burning conviction fanned it into life.

Royal dignity may not have come within her range –'Her art, supreme as it is', remarked Clement Scott, 'can never conceal the passionate Bohemian'– but one observer long treasured a moment of 'magical and almost supernatural beauty' as she stepped slowly down the landing-stage for her first meeting with Mark Antony. She was, by turns, coaxing, flattering, languishing, then petulant, bored, passionate, reaching a climax in the scene where, in a towering rage, she attacked the slave who brought the news of Antony's marriage, then proceeded to wreck the palace in her jealous fury. But in the death scene she slipped into death without dwelling on harrowing details, though she did allow herself the indulgence of a real snake to give the audience a final *frisson*.

Meticulous about detail, Bernhardt concocted her own body make-up from saffron and powdered Mocha coffee, combined with chicory and musk, and diluted with rosewater. She even made up the palms of her hands, which would never be noticed across the footlights. *The Lady's Newspaper* revealed that each costume consisted of '7 yards' length of some diaphanous and clinging material, wrapped with consummate art round the lithesome form of the actress, and cunningly held together at the neck and waist with gorgeous stones of every possible shade'.

Ellen Terry noted that Bernhardt gave the picture of an emotion, never the emotion itself. Bernhardt's were studied interpretations, given life by the blazing intensity of her exotic, bohemian temperament. Her greatest asset was her voice –'a soft chant, little above a whisper, yet of a penetrating and bewildering sweetness' that not even the crudities of contemporary recordings can destroy. She dominated the theatre for over fifty years, her splendour almost undimmed to the end, still hypnotizing audiences by the power of her imagination as 'they sat open-mouthed, her slaves; lesser entities bowing at the court of tempestuous purpose'. *(SW)*

Sarah Bernhardt [Bernard] (1845–1923), French actress, who made her début at the Comédie-Française in 1862. She was noted for her interpretations in French classic drama, especially in Racine's *Phèdre*, and in other plays such as *Hamlet*, Dumas's *La Dame aux camélias*, Sardou's *La Tosca*, and Rostand's *L'Aiglon*. She managed a number of Paris theatres, naming one after herself, and toured extensively, especially to London and the USA.

Sarah Bernhardt in the title role of *Cléopâtre*
Photograph by Sarony, 1891
Guy Little Collection

I lift my hat to Mr. Novello. He can wade through tosh with the straightest face; the tongue never visibly approaches the cheek. Both as actor and as author he can pursue adventures too preposterous even for the films and do it with that solemn fixity of purpose which romantic drama inexorably demands.

IVOR BROWN REVIEWING **GLAMOROUS NIGHT** (**THE OBSERVER,** 5 MAY 1935)

By 1935 Ivor Novello was famous as an actor on stage and screen, and as a playwright and songwriter. *Glamorous Night* was, however, the first time all his talents came together to create a musical play – starring himself. To the tradition of the spectacular melodramas and pantomimes for which Drury Lane was famous Novello now added his own touch of the romantic musical, and the result was a unique mixture of melodrama, operetta, and musical comedy, with twenty spectacular scenes – and a minimal plot.

Against a background of Ruritanian-style politics, an Englishman meets a king's mistress, they run away together, and in the end she renounces love for duty. This action incorporated two assassination attempts, a rampaging mob, a shipboard cabaret, a liner sinking in full view of the audience, a mountain trek, a gypsy wedding, a dungeon rescue, and the televising of a royal wedding. The settings included a suburban London street, the futuristic office of a radio tycoon, several rooms in Krasnian noble houses, the Krasnian state opera house, an ocean liner, a mountain range, a gypsy encampment, the castle of Borvnik, the Palace of Krasnia, and a television studio.

Nerman's cartoon opposite is in stark contrast to all the spectacle and romance, but it captures one of the most effective points of the plot. Mary Ellis, as befitting her role as Militza, gipsy-born opera singer mistress of the King of Krasnia, was allowed a flamboyant manner. In contrast, Novello, as Anthony Allen, was an unromantic hero with an offhand, rather impertinent manner, and their love scenes were played out as light comedy or quarrels.

Novello's most effective entrance of the evening came when, having saved the life of the King of Krasnia, he arrived to be decorated for his services to the state, a lonely figure in a dark lounge suit amid the colour and splendour of the Krasnian court. Mary Ellis, too, was not denied her moments. She had a superb last exit as, 'turning her back on her audience and on love, in her gorgeous gown with its sweeping train, she mounted slowly but steadily a long staircase treading the path of duty, leaving love behind'. The play had the most gratifying effect on its audiences, reducing even Queen Mary to tears. *(SW)*

Ivor Novello [David Ivor Davies] (1893–1951), Welsh actor, dramatist, composer, and film star who first achieved fame in 1914 with the song 'Keep the Home Fires Burning', made his stage début in 1921, and in the 1930s made Drury Lane his centre with a hit series of his own musicals: *Glamorous Night* (1935), *Careless Rapture* (1936), *Crest of the Wave* (1937), and *The Dancing Years* (1939). Post-war successes included *Perchance to Dream* (1945) and *King's Rhapsody* (1949). **Mary Ellis** (b. 1901), American actress, singer, and film star who made her stage début at the Metropolitan Opera, New York, in 1918, and later created the title role in the musical play *Rose-Marie* (1924). Following her success in the stage and film versions of *Glamorous Night* with *The Dancing Years* (1939), she later starred in a wide range of popular roles and in classics by Shakespeare, Sheridan, O'Neill, and Shaw.

Ivor Novello as Anthony Allen and **Mary Ellis** as
Militza in *Glamorous Night* (Theatre Royal, Drury
Lane, 1935)
Einar Nerman
Original artwork for *The Illustrated Sporting and Dramatic
News*, 31 May 1935
Pen and ink 382 × 572
Lent by Mary Ellis

He is beautiful and bloody; he is the Germ of Destruction, the Spirit of Unrest.
. . . It is terrible but it is magnificent; it is barbarous, it is the alpha and
omega of human existence; for it is war.

ARTHUR APPLIN (**THE STORIES OF THE RUSSIAN BALLET**, 1911)

On 19 May 1909 a sophisticated audience of an evening of Russian ballet organized by Serge Diaghilev settled into their seats after an elegant evocation of eighteenth-century France in *Le Pavillon d'Armide* starring the young Nijinsky (see No. 1). But when the curtain rose on the next item in the programme, an excerpt from Borodin's opera *Prince Igor*, nothing could have seemed more alien to Parisian eyes. Roerich's set transported them to the Russian steppes: tribal huts smoking against an ochre sky, brooding, desolate, barbaric. To entertain the captive Prince Igor, the Khan summoned his slave girls and warriors. On to the stage erupted a wild, barbaric horde 'ferocious of aspect, their faces smeared with soot and mud'.

Into the midst of this highly-choreographed disorder leapt Adolph Bolm as the Warrior Chief, dancing as if possessed: in him was symbolized the 'spontaneity, passion, and proud freedom of the nomadic tribes', far divorced from the civilized Russo-European St. Petersburg. The pounding rhythms of Borodin's music, the sustained chanting of the chorus, the ferocious savagery of Fokine's choreography whipped the audience into a virtual frenzy, and the overpowering climax came as Bolm swept towards the audience, spun in the air, and, as the curtain fell, crashed onto one knee, at the same time loosing his bow.

No one in that Paris audience could have imagined a man dancing in such a wild, uninhibited way: the male dancer had become a figure of ridicule, tolerated, if at all, only as a partner, his roles being taken by a shapely girl *en travesti*. Almost overnight Bolm redressed the balance, and the male dancer was restored to his rightful place as at least the equal of the ballerina.

Frödman-Cluzel's bronze conveys the style of the ballet and also Bolm's physique, which conditioned Fokine's choreography. His heavy feet he used to crash onto the ground and emphasize the rhythm and ferocity of the music, while the proud curve of the body, the defiant turn of the head, capture the character of the tribal warrior. Not least of the revolutions wrought by the Diaghilev Ballet in its early years was that it reasserted the infinite variety of style and expression inherent within ballet and its validity as an expressive theatrical medium. *(SW)*

Adolph Bolm (1884–1951), Russian dancer, choreographer, and teacher, who later became a naturalized American. He joined the Maryinsky Theatre in 1903, danced with Diaghilev's company during its first Paris season, and in 1911 left the Maryinsky to join Diaghilev's company permanently. Deciding to stay in the USA, he worked for the Metropolitan Opera, New York, and the Chicago Civic Opera, to become one of the great pioneer figures of the American ballet scene.

Adolph Bolm as the Warrior Chief in Polovtsian Dances
from *Prince Igor*
B. B. Frödman-Cluzel, 1909
Bronze Height: 243
Cyril Beaumont Collection

The musical-box is going splendidly and is my delight, because when I am singing well I give myself much pleasure without knowing that sometimes I am giving pleasure to others too.

CARUSO TO SYBIL SELIGMAN (IN V. SELIGMAN, **PUCCINI AMONG FRIENDS,** 1938)

Enrico Caruso was always concerned about the health of his 'musical-box' and regularly sprayed his tonsils with a special solution. Although he took great pains with his acting, it was the quality of the voice, 'gold swathed in velvet', which overcame the slightly ridiculous appearance of the stocky Neapolitan on stage. This was even more apparent because many of his wide range of tenor roles had previously been sung by the handsome Polish tenor, Jean de Reszke. Melba, who partnered both in succession, was devoted to de Reszke, but even she liked singing with Caruso and said of his voice: 'The higher he sings the more easy it seems to him'.

The Duke of Mantua in Verdi's opera *Rigoletto* was Caruso's début at Covent Garden in 1902, as later in New York and Paris. The Duke is a heartless seducer whose courtship of Gilda, his court jester's daughter, leads to tragedy when his courtiers abduct her. To save the Duke from her father's murderous revenge, Gilda substitutes herself and dies for her love.

Caruso's voice darkened over the years, and though he continued to sing the role of the Duke with success he considered the part no longer right for him. He became increasingly interested in the heavier character parts such as Eleazar in *La Juive*, the last role he ever sang. He was in much pain while singing Eleazar, but he was such a conscientious artist that he would rarely cancel a performance, even if risking his health. This reliability, together with his effortless voice, made him an extremely popular singer, and he also endeared himself to his audience – if not always to other singers – by his sense of humour.

One of Caruso's most outstanding contributions to the history of opera was his early acceptance of the gramophone as an important new medium. His many recordings made him a legend in his own time, for they brought to a far wider public his voice 'of such endurance and responsiveness', and also encouraged other artists to record. *(CEH)*

Enrico Caruso (1873–1921), Italian tenor, born in Naples, the dark tone of whose voice caused him to be regarded as a baritone in his early years. He made his début in Morelli's *L'amico francesco* in 1894, and first sang at Covent Garden in *Rigoletto* in 1902, but appeared more often at the Metropolitan Opera, New York, where he gave his last performance in Halévy's *La Juive* in 1920.

Enrico Caruso as the Duke of Mantua in *Rigoletto*
Photograph by Ellis and Walery
Gabrielle Enthoven Collection

With a curious quick shuffling movement of her feet, she makes her
apparently motionless body move rapidly over the stage, cutting sizeable
geometric squares from its surface; and what seems to be a miracle has
happened, for the squares are no longer cut from the floor but from measureless
Western areas and the theatre is filled with a sense of speed and travel and wind.

ROY HARGRAVE ON MARTHA GRAHAM IN **FRONTIER**, 1935
(AS QUOTED IN ARLENE CROCE, **AFTERIMAGES**, 1978)

A 'tribute to the vision and independence of the pioneer woman as she carved out her destiny in the new land' was the programme note to *Frontier* but, typically of Martha Graham's work, the dance in performance suggested other frontiers of physical and spiritual strength in the American pioneer woman. This was one of many aspects of woman's life that Graham was to enshrine in her choreography over the years: woman as participant in wars and migrations as creator, destroyer, as wife, mistress, mother, queen, saint, unnamed in the early years but later taking on specific identities – Emily Dickinson, the Brontës, Herodias, then Clytemnestra, Medea, Mary Queen of Scots, Joan of Arc.

Like Isadora Duncan (see No. 26) before her, Graham rejected formal dance training and evolved her own technique, finding, again like Duncan, the solar plexus as the mainspring from which all movement would come.

The photograph opposite shows the flexible back and body demanded by the Graham style, as opposed to the relative rigidity of the body in classical ballet, and the extraordinary extension of the limbs which is a hallmark of her style. In common with other modern dance forms, the Graham technique has explored 'falls' and the relationship of the body to the ground – unlike classical ballet, where the impetus is the defiance of gravity and the impulse is to escape from the earth.

The severe simplicity of the costume is another Graham hallmark. By cut and style, its plainness becomes at one with the body, and hence an integral part of the dance and the movement, creating its own patterns, which are nevertheless dictated by the overall pattern of the dance.

From the beginning of her career, Graham was able to formulate her ideas into a definable technique, and this formed the foundation of a company and a school. Her technique creates a body flexible enough to serve choreographic ideas of all kinds, all emotions, and all characters, and which is capable of growth as different demands are made upon it. Thus her work, unlike Duncan's, has outlasted her own dancing life and her roles live on in a new generation of dancers, here represented by Janet Eilber. *(SW)*

Martha Graham (b. 1894), American dancer, choreographer, teacher, and founder and director of the Martha Graham Dance Company. She gave her first solo recital in New York in 1926, to become the foremost exponent of modern dance in America. Her ballets include *Letter to the World* (1940), *Appalachian Spring* (1944), *Errand into the Maze* (1947), *Diversion of Angels* (1948) and *Clytemnestra* (1958). **Janet Eilber** (b. 1951), American dancer who joined the Martha Graham Company in 1972, performing almost every major role in the repertory. She has also appeared with the Joffrey Ballet and the American Dance Machine.

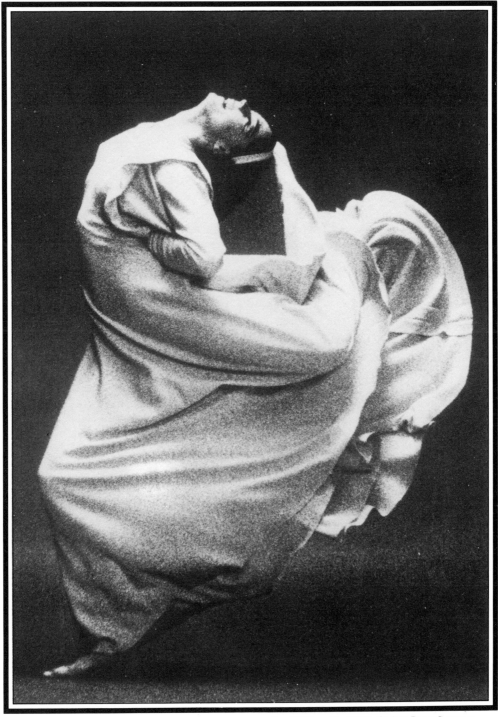

Janet Eilber of the Martha Graham Dance Company
in *Frontier*
Photograph by Max Waldman
© Max Waldman 1976. All rights reserved

Among Edwardian musical comedies, *The Arcadians* was outstanding not only for its tuneful score and above-average story, but for its realistic scenic effects – and there was also a good helping of comedy to season an otherwise sugary offering. The scene is Askwood racecourse. Suddenly, in the middle of the meeting, strange beings clad in pseudo-Greek draperies arrive amid the fashionable racegoers. They are Arcadians, who have come to England to 'set up the truth for ever more and banish the lie'.

Among them is Simplicitas – in fact plain Mr. Smith, who in Act I has been transformed into a young and handsome Arcadian. Before long he meets Mrs. Smith, and she falls in love with the young stranger, not recognizing him as her husband –'which gives rise to much comic "business" between Mr. Dan Rolyat and Miss Ada Blanche', as a reviewer noted with satisfaction. The main love-interest, between Eileen Cavanagh and Jack Meadows, was in the safe hands of Phyllis Dare and Harry Welchman, with Florence Smithson, 'who bears herself like a Peri and sings like an angel', as the Arcadian who causes their temporary estrangement. All was, of course, explained before the final curtain, when the Arcadians return to Arcadia, their mission a failure, but leaving behind Simplicitas, once more transformed into prosaic Mr. Smith.

The Arcadians is one of a distinguished group of musicals, to which *Oklahoma!* also belongs, in which few people had faith during rehearsals – even one of the composers, Lionel Monckton, assured a rival manager that 'it hasn't a chance'. But Robert Courtneidge, who was making his first venture into London management, never realized that everybody was anticipating failure – though looking back he was not surprised, for he remembered that, beyond the particular situations that concerned them, the composers knew nothing about the play, a situation hard to envisage today when 'integrated' musicals and close collaboration is the norm.

Courtneidge's faith was justified. *The Arcadians* became one of the most successful musical comedies of its day, and ran for two years. Unlike many of its contemporaries, it is still performed occasionally by amateur operatic societies, and the overture and the songs 'Arcady' and 'The Pipes of Pan' have remained standard numbers in the light music repertory. *(SW)*

Ada Blanche as Mrs. Smith and **Dan Rolyat** as
Simplicitas in *The Arcadians* (Shaftesbury Theatre,
London, 1909)
Photograph by Foulsham and Banfield

Danny Kaye . . . is a whirlwind of sound and movement. His tongue, lips and larynx release a cascade of jumping, tumbling, rhythmic words; his blue eyes roll, blink, flutter, shut and pop; his sensitive, slender hands wave, gyrate, caress, and syncopate; his long legs bounce and dance.

MILTON SHULMAN (**EVENING STANDARD**, 6 FEBRUARY 1948)

Danny Kaye's first appearance at the London Palladium in February 1948 was 'the biggest individual variety success in London for many years', and during the six-week season more than a quarter of a million people came to see him, creating a black market in theatre tickets. For the following season all the tickets were sold in advance, and hundreds slept on the pavements outside in the hope of obtaining standing room. He topped the bill at the Royal Command Performance in November 1949, when he persuaded the royal party to join in his nonsense songs.

Danny Kaye once said that he could not be funny 'in a room'. On stage he captivated audiences for an hour or more with his intimate chats, marvellously enunciated 'gobble-degook' songs, and skittish dancing. His puckish humour contrasted with a casually elegant appearance, and his act was executed with unbounded energy and fast changes of mood and sense. Kaye's timing was superb, and an apparently 'spontaneous' performance developed from detailed planning and rehearsal. He could hold the rapt attention of an audience while sitting on the stage drinking a cup of tea.

The photograph shows Kaye hopping and singing behind the microphone – an instrument which he never allowed to get in his way, but reduced 'to its proper place as a mere stage prop which enables him to make intimate contact with a larger audience' (W. A. Darlington). He created brilliantly funny effects from the juxtaposition of the illogical and the mundane, as when singing about 'Jakob Herzheimderbofhausvonkleinstorpdaswetteristgemutlichderpfeifeldienkehkehvonausterlitzeindadaeindada (pause) Junior'. Only Kaye *could* sing that.

Kaye's natural flair as a performer was evident at an early age, and his talent for movement was disciplined by the dancers Dave Harvey and Kathleen Young, who met him when he was appearing in a vaudeville troupe in the early 1930s. Those who never saw him in person can judge from his recordings and films the truth of the statement: 'If Danny Kaye had not been born, no one could possibly have invented him'. *(CH)*

Danny Kaye [David Daniel Kaminski] (b. 1913), American comedian and film star, born in Brooklyn, who first joined a vaudeville troupe in 1933. A successful appearance at a New York nightclub in 1940 singing songs by the pianist and lyricist Sylvia Fine led to their marriage in 1941. In the same year he made his name on Broadway appearing in *Lady in the Dark* with Gertrude Lawrence, and starring in *Let's Face It*. His first film, *Up in Arms* (1944), led to a long succession of films for the producer Samuel Goldwyn and much work in television.

Danny Kaye (London Palladium, 1948)
Photograph: Keystone Press Agency

No puppet performs by itself. If [the puppeteer] does not continue to give attention, everything slumps. Awareness of the puppet is more necessary to the puppeteer than of his body to the actor. . . . The puppet cannot think unless the puppeteer thinks too.

JOHN HOUGHMASTER

A good puppet performance offers pleasure on several levels. There is conscious pleasure in the virtuosity of the operator, whose skill and agility make or mar a performance; intellectual pleasure in the treatment of the subject; and the sheer joy of the spectacle, with its contrasts, colours, sounds, and harmonies. The kinds of puppetry to which we are most accustomed are the glove puppet with its booth and the marionette – a jointed puppet operated by strings. Most people know glove puppets through Punch and Judy; marionettes have perhaps become less widely accessible, probably because they perform in their own, less portable theatres. But in both cases it is only over the past century or so that puppets have become almost exclusively an entertainment for children, though new developments in puppetry are changing this image.

Opposite is illustrated *Starchild* (1973), a modern production which introduces different types of puppets. The story is an updated version of the Grimm brothers' tale, *The Giant with the Three Golden Hairs*. A young boy survives the dangerous quest of fetching three golden hairs from the head of a giant, thereby winning wisdom, maturity, and the hand of the king's daughter. The giant is actually a live actor in a mask seated on a step-ladder; he acts alongside rod-puppets, such as the grandmother on the right, whose operator is just visible in the picture. The rod in the right hand of the operator controls and guides her right arm as she moves forward to steal one of the giant's hairs, while his left hand controls the movements of her head and body.

The operators of rod-puppets are visible to the audience, as in Japanese Bunraku puppetry, and here they are clothed from head to toe in off-white, in the same tone as the backdrop. Sometimes their skill in movement is such that they become co-ordinated blocks of movement giving their individuality to the puppets they control. The truth and liveliness thus imparted spring from a minute observation of human movement, and a sense of pleasurable discovery and enriched imagination arises from the fusion and development of eastern and western puppetry traditions into a spectacle to reach everyone. As Barry Smith and Alan Judd have said, the puppet theatre 'can be a rendezvous, a "gathering together" of different classes and age groups. It shares with circuses, mime, magicians, and the comics of silent film the power to dissolve barriers between adult, adolescent, and child – each revealing to the other a different aspect of a shared experience'. *(ER)*

Barry Smith's Theatre of Puppets performing *Starchild*
Photograph by Barry Smith

Ever seen his eyes? The saddest eyes in the whole world. That's why we all laughed at Danny. Because if we hadn't laughed, we should have cried ourselves sick. I believe that's what real comedy is, you know. It's almost like crying.

MARIE LLOYD (QUOTED IN GYLES BRANDRETH, **THE FUNNIEST MAN ON EARTH,** 1977)

From his first appearance at 'The Lane' in 1888 until his death in 1904, Dan Leno and the Drury Lane pantomime were linked in the public mind. By the end of the century pantomime had developed into the entertainment we would recognize today – with its emphasis on lavish spectacle, and on 'star' names, recruited, like Leno, from the music halls. Leno was, above all, the supreme pantomime dame, but in 1894 at Drury Lane he played Idle Jack in *Dick Whittington*. Especially remembered was his monologue when, about to marry the heroine, he waited at the church, intoxicated, impatient, and increasingly manic, building up a piece of monumental verbal absurdity that, delivered in his unique, intimate staccato style, was irresistible.

Leno's face, 'with all the tragedy that is writ on the face of a baby monkey', as Max Beerbohm described it, combined sorrowful, almost reproachful eyes with the pained surprise of the arched eyebrows. The wise, expressive mouth suggested a traditional clown's sadness or a wide mischievous grin, but never lost a sense of strain. The body was consciously placed, from the 'disconcerting legs' to a carefully held handkerchief and stick – not a confident pose, but revealing a wariness of the surrounding world. In this as in his comedy patter Leno reflected with painstaking fidelity the drudgery that made up the lives of the music-hall's predominantly working-class audience. He expressed that audience's grievances, and came to symbolize their indomitable spirit and will to survive.

Leno developed an intimate, gossipy style, establishing an extraordinary rapport with his audience until he conjured up from his own imagination 'whole breadths of London . . . all the flickering street corners on Saturday nights, all the world of crowded door-steps and open windows' (M. Willson Disher). *(SW)*

Dan Leno [George Galvin] (1860–1904), English music-hall artist, on the stage from the age of four, world champion clog dancer at twenty, and subsequently one of the leading music-hall performers of his day. Nicknamed 'The King's Jester' following his Royal Command performance in 1901, he returned to the stage after his mental health broke down in 1903, but died the following year, aged 43.

Dan Leno as Idle Jack in *Dick Whittington*
Photograph by Hana
Guy Little Collection

> We are making our own statement – others are making more intellectual ones.
> I'm not a spokesman for the immorality of our world. I'm a singer . . .
> a performer.
>
> MICK JAGGER (IN J. MARKS, **MICK JAGGER – THE SINGER, NOT THE SONG**, 1974)

Rock's archetypal showman, Mick Jagger can stimulate an audience to unique peaks and depths. Much of his consummate professionalism is built on hype, but the narcissistic Lucifer he creates on stage has been relentlessly rehearsed in front of the mirror. Those famous lips, on which David Oxtoby's etching so lovingly dwells, have always been used for more than lyrics. The combination of artifice and honesty that goes into performance applies to the songs of the Rolling Stones as well. Mick may sing 'I Can't Get No Satisfaction', but we know that he can – and he does.

Jagger and Keith Richard followed the blues rockers Chuck Berry and Bo Diddley, while Brian Jones was an *aficionado* of blues purists such as Elmore James. This amalgam resulted in the ultimate contradiction of a bunch of white English middle-class boys playing black working-class American music. The resultant frustrations of not being Negro were transmuted into the emotional range of rage, pathos, and sexual aggression in the early 1960s recordings, and instigated the genre of white rhythm and blues which outraged the jazz establishment of 1963.

Deliberately setting out to woo kids by alienating their parents, as stage-door riots were succeeded by BBC bannings and public urination, the Rolling Stones won an unsurpassed reputation for unmitigated evil. Yet they were not revolutionaries – and, at the height of their persecution, with Jagger under jail sentence for a ludicrously minor drug offence, *The Times* came to the rescue with an apposite editorial, 'Who Breaks a Butterfly on a Wheel?', showing considerable sympathy for the devil. Public rehabilitation had begun.

· Eventually, in spite of lukewarm tributes to 'The Salt of the Earth', their final analysis of the rock revolution became: 'what else can a poor boy do but to join in a rock 'n' roll band?'. The Stones' commitment to the blues became stronger than that to streetfighting, and Mick Jagger's commitment to performance became greater than both. *(DF)*

The Rolling Stones, formed 1962, first performed at the Marquee Club in 1962. 'Come On', their first single, encouraged Lennon and McCartney to write the Stones a top twenty hit 'I Wanna Be Your Man' (1963). A string of hugely successful singles (such as 'Satisfaction' (1965) and 'Paint It Black' (1966)) and albums ('Out Of Our Heads' (1965) and 'Aftermath' (1966)) followed, but the later 1960s and early 1970s were characterized by scandal, persecution, and tragedy. 'Beggars Banquet' (1968), 'Let It Bleed' (1969), and 'Exile On Main Street' (1972) maintained for a while their excellence on record, but the 1970s saw The Rolling Stones sinking into complacency, only their live performances retaining vigour, though a flirtation with disco sounds in 'Some Girls' (1978) showed signs of a new direction.

Mick Jagger
'Jaggin', one of fifteen portraits of rock stars,
Twentieth Century Musicians and Singers
David Oxtoby
Published by J. C. Editions, 1974
Etching, No. 42 in an edition of 50, 293 × 190
[S.461–1980]

PRODUCTION
PROCESSES

Sitting through the rehearsals of his play *In Celebration* at the Royal Court in 1969, David Storey became increasingly bored by 'the endless arrangement of cups and saucers, the laying down and taking up of coats and bags. . .'. The pre-occupation with technicalities left him no opportunity to discuss what the play was 'about'. It was only when watching a preview performance four weeks later that he suddenly realized, as he explains, that 'the "mechanics" of the rehearsals were . . . the medium through which experience, not in an abstract sense, but in all its particularities, could be discovered'.

Unless a dramatist directs his own play, he passes the responsibility for translating it into concrete terms to a director. Casting is one of the first things to be sorted out, for on it much of the success of the production will hang – 60 per cent, according to Arnold Wesker. Obviously, one's initial choice of actors might well be those whose other commitments make them unavailable, and so compromises have to be made. Many interviews, auditions, and negotiations – either direct or through artists' agents – may take place before contracts are signed; and in large organizations such as the Royal Shakespeare Company and the National Theatre casting directors are employed to deal with these administrative problems. Written agreements between actor and management are of ancient standing. It was standard practice in the medieval theatre for actors to sign contracts, promising under threat of fine to attend rehearsals and performances, perhaps also binding themselves not to exchange parts without permission, argue with the producer, or get drunk.

Another aspect of production to be determined early on is the stage setting. To Peter Brook this is crucial to his thinking about a play. As he said of his production of *King Lear* in 1962: 'I am absolutely incapable of solving a production other than through the scenery. The set is a summing up of everything that one has felt and studied in a production . . . like an "essence" of the play which, if it's wrong, defeats you all the time. The well-designed set opens all possibilities. . . .' Although Brook designed his own set for *King Lear*, it is more usual for a director to work in close association with a stage designer – a relationship which may endure for many productions. John Bury describes how his designs for Peter Hall's productions will start out from a key-image: 'Peter will say "steel" – and you go away and think what that means. . .'.

The designer is not only concerned with what the sets will look like, but whether they can be constructed within the budget and time schedule; whether they can be changed quickly, now that lengthy scene changes are no longer the norm; and whether the materials to be used conform to fire regulations. Nowadays the same designer is usually also responsible for properties, masks, wigs, and costumes. He must have intimate knowledge of fabrics and how they respond to movement (particularly where dancers are concerned), and of how different dyes react under artificial light.

Providing drawings that clearly convey colour, line, and detail is only part of the job. When Alan Barlow designs costumes he chooses 'personally, their fabrics, braids, buttons, linings, decoration; decides their pattern and cut; attends to period detail, accuracy and research; selects or designs jewellery, shoes, boots, scarves, belts, shawls, gloves, fans, fobs, furs, and furbelows. . .'. Since the designer must ensure that his designs work in practice, he will liaise closely with the workshops and attend costume fittings and rehearsals.

Much of the design is planned in detail before rehearsals begin, leaving as much time as possible for construction and modification. In recent decades there have been attempts, notably by Joan Littlewood with Theatre Workshop at Stratford East, to delay the design process to coincide with rehearsals, a method that well suits experimental theatre groups with low overheads who may create their scripts through improvisation. It is also frequently the practice in ballet, where the designer observes the creation of the 'script' by the choreographer in rehearsals before setting to work. At the first rehearsal of most plays, however, the costume designs and groundplan of the set will be shown to the cast by the director, together with the three-dimensional model which acts as a guide for the company and workshops.

How rehearsals are conducted varies according to the director – or producer, as he was generally known from his emergence in the nineteenth century until relatively recent years. Few are likely to be as eccentric as those of Herbert Beerbohm Tree, as Oscar Asche recalls: 'Tree never seemed inclined to work till after midnight . . . [he] would look in just before lunch for about ten minutes. His next appearance would be about nine, after dinner. He would then rehearse for two hours, and then to supper. About 1 a.m. he would turn up, fresh and cheery, and say: "Come, let's do some *work!*".'

Some directors may prefer to begin rehearsals with physical exercises or with formal readings, or to discuss the play and its background, or to proceed immediately with 'blocking out' the actors' movements. John Dexter, according to Jim Hiley's account of the production, spent the first week of his rehearsals for *Galileo* at the National Theatre in 1980 running through the blocking he had prepared in advance. Other directors, such as Jonathan Miller and Clifford Williams, dislike preparing moves before rehearsals begin. The stage design may also have to be adapted as a result of the blocking process.

While coaching the performers, the director at the same time co-ordinates the technical side of the production – the stage management, sound, and lighting cues. If a lighting designer is not available, the lighting is worked out with the chief electrician either by the director or the set designer. A lighting designer will discuss the production with the director, and the colours and fabrics used with the designer, before making charts recording the positions and timings of the actors on stage. Lighting can then be pencilled in, first in black and white, then in colour in preparation for the actual focusing of the lamps.

It is only at the end of the production process that the various elements which the director has held in his head start to come together. Once the set is built, lighting cues, costume changes, and sound effects are run through in the technical rehearsals before the dress rehearsals with the actors. As the final deadline approaches, the pressure on the director can be particularly intense, especially if he undertakes the leading role in his own production. Of his *Macbeth* production John Gielgud wrote to his designer Michael Ayrton in 1942: 'The technical side of a big production depends greatly on too many different people, and the handling of all the departments is always a tricky and full-time job, quite apart from the more personal agonies of seeing the finished work, judging it, lighting, bearing criticism, and then becoming so familiar and stale with it all that one loses all sense of judgement of knowledge of the final worth . . .' (letter in the Theatre Museum's collection).

Although the imminence of the audience may be disquieting at the final dress rehearsal, an audience can help focus the actor's performance, as Simon Callow observes:

'They tell the story back to you. They experience the story you have in a way forgotten, and let you know how well you're telling it'. Hence, perhaps, the recent development of 'preview' performances, open to the public. But most of the effort of mounting a production is still in preparation for the official 'first night'. And when the run is over the sense of participation can be particularly nostalgic, as David Suchet found when he witnessed the 'get-out' of the National Youth Theatre's *Bartholomew Fair* from the Royal Court in 1966: 'All the scenery was coming down and the lights were being taken out and the costumes put away and I remember thinking how strange it was that something we had all made real a few hours earlier was all coming apart on pieces of canvas. I could hear the echo of the audience laughter, and the atmosphere was so strong that I thought the theatre was really where I wanted always to be, putting it back together again'. *(JF)*

'The fact is, Mr. R., I have been nineteen years endeavouring to satisfy my own taste in this play, and have not yet succeeded.' This was Sheridan's reply to the publisher James Ridgeway, who bought the option on *The School for Scandal* in about 1799 and was waiting for the final corrections that Sheridan had promised to send. Sheridan was both a perfectionist and a procrastinator, as is evident from the fact that he still wanted to revise the play years after its first production at Drury Lane, on 8 May 1777. He never completed his promised revisions, and after Ridgeway 'expostulated pretty strongly' with him for keeping him waiting, Ridgeway abandoned his plans to publish.

Richard Brinsley Sheridan (1751–1816) was manager of Drury Lane when his play was first performed there. It was a great success, and, since he wanted to ensure that other companies could not easily obtain copies of the text, he resisted publication of the play until 1781, when the first English edition appeared. By this date an Irish company had already obtained a pirated version, and some prompt-copies appear to have been made for provincial companies, both with and without Sheridan's consent.

About a dozen drafts and finished manuscripts of *The School for Scandal* are extant, some in Sheridan's hand and others penned by scribes. Sheridan corrected some of the copies, adding and deleting in his characteristic handwriting. The page illustrated here is from an early scribal manuscript which Sheridan worked over, and contains the character Miss Verjuice who later became Snake, Lady Sneerwell's obsequious servant. The way in which Sheridan changed his mind about the text can be seen from his alterations, such as the deletion of 'They were' in Snake's first speech, which he changed to 'He did'– before inserting 'They were' again.

Working from memory, Sheridan often forgot to carry corrections on from one text to another, and no two manuscripts are identical. Neither did he see any reason to consider his texts sacrosanct after their first performance. As he wrote in his preface to *The Rivals*: 'For my own part I see no reason why the Author of a play should not regard a First Night's audience as a candid and judicious friend attending, in behalf of the public, at his last Rehearsal'.

Sheridan composed in haste and revised at leisure. He wrote the first version of *The School for Scandal* in two months, but never completed a final text of it to his own satisfaction. One day during the initial composition 'the under-writer was vibrating to the theatre from his [Sheridan's] house, and back again, like a pendulum: and, as Mahomet with the Alcoran, received it only a sheet at a time, to enable the copyist to get on with the parts destined to the actors to study from'. *(CH)*

Act 1st: Scene 1st:

Lady Sneerwell's House)

Lady Sneerwell at the Dressing Table)

drinking Chocolate.

L: Sneer
The Pharagraphs, were all inserted?

Snake:
They were Madam; and as I copied them my
self in a feign'd hand, there can be no suspicion
whence they came.

L: Sneer:
Did you circulate the Report of Lady Brittles
Intrigue wt: Capt. Boastall.

Madam by this time Lady Brittle is the talk
of half the Town — and I doubt not but in
a Week the Men will toast her as a Demi
-rep

L: Sneer
What have you done as to the insinuation
of a certain Baronets Lady and a certain Earl

That is in as fine a train as yr: Ladyship:

Script. Opening page from an early draft of
The School for Scandal, first produced 1777.
Anonymous scribe, with alterations by Sheridan
Manuscript 224 × 184
British Theatre Museum Association

In preparation for a new stage production many copies of the script are annotated. The author may make revisions or add directions to the original drafts, the director and the stage management add notes to their copies, and performers mark cues and comments. Until 1968 other familiar marks seen on playscripts were the blue-pencil deletions made by the Lord Chamberlain's Examiner of Plays.

The page opposite, with its blue cross and red stamp, comes from the licensed script of *Revudeville No. 33*, produced at the Windmill Theatre on 11 September 1933. The revue as a whole was deemed fit for public performance by the Lord Chamberlain provided that this and one other sketch were deleted – *The Burglar* being cut not because nudity was revealed but because it was *active* nudity. The Windmill had featured nudes in their popular non-stop revues since these began in 1931, but only nudes in tableaux were permitted.

Dramatic censorship had existed since the reign of Henry VII, but this dealt primarily with sensitive political and religious references in plays. Dramatists' freedom was further restricted by the Licensing Act of 1737, and by the Theatres Act of 1843, which stated that: 'No profanity or impropriety of language; no indecency of dress, dance or gesture; and no offensive personalities or representations of living persons are permitted on the stage'. Every play had to be submitted to the Lord Chamberlain's office not less than seven days before its first performance, and refusal to implement required alterations could result in prosecution.

Nineteenth-century playwrights, including W. S. Gilbert and G. B. Shaw, repeatedly voiced their frustration at the powers of the Lord Chamberlain, Shaw calling him: 'one who robs, insults and suppresses me as irresistibly as if he were the Tsar of Russia and I the meanest of his subjects'. In the 1960s David Mercer talked about 'the tedium of trading four-letter words with the gentlemen play examiners of Stable Yard, St. James's Palace', noting that 'bugger is disallowed but a fart or two is handed back by way of consolation'.

In July 1968 the Lord Chamberlain himself put forward reasons why theatrical censorship was 'no longer appropriate', and the Theatres Act abolishing it came into force on 26 September 1968. The following evening *Hair* opened at the Shaftesbury Theatre, and dimly lit but undeniably moving nude bodies were at last legally seen on the London stage. Although prior censorship of scripts has thus been abolished, Peter Hall, director of the National Theatre, complained in 1981 of 'censorship by subsidy', which threatens subsidized theatres with loss of (or a cut in) their grant for presenting material considered indecent. In that year the director of the National Theatre production of Howard Brenton's *The Romans in Britain*, Michael Bogdanov, was committed to stand trial at the Old Bailey as a result of a private prosecution, accused under the Sexual Offences Act (1956) of procuring two actors to simulate a homosexual rape on stage. The indeterminate outcome of the eventual trial left the theatre once more uncertain of the limits of its freedom from censorship. *(CH)*

"THE BURGLAR"

Characters:

The Lady
The Burglar.

Scene - A lady's bedroom.

The sketch opens with a deserted stage. A girl's

voice can be heard off-stage singing, as if in her bath.

A very tough looking character enters from the side and peers

furtively about. He sees the dressing table and goes quickly

over to it. As he is bending over a jewel-case on it, a girl

enters through the doorway at the back. She has just got

out of her bath and is wearing only a towel, which she is

holding round herself. She walks a couple of paces into the

room before she becomes aware of the burglar, who simultaneously

turns and sees her. He whips out a revolver from his pocket.

Burglar: (Fiercely)   'Ands up!

The Girl screams and begins to raise both hands -

        BLACK OUT.

Censored script. A sketch, *The Burglar*, deleted by the
Examiner of Plays at the Lord Chamberlain's Office,
from *Revudeville No.* 33 (1933)
Typescript 253 × 203
Given by Sheila Van Damm

If you had been casting a play in 1952 you might well have consulted *The Spotlight Casting Directory for Stage and Screen* – then as now the indispensable shop window for the artists and stage personnel it publicizes. First published in 1927 in single-volume form, it quickly grew into a two-volume edition – one for actors and one for actresses and children – issued twice yearly. In 1974, after the men's section had been further split into two volumes and the women's and children's section divided to make four volumes in all, publication was limited to once a year.

Artists appear alphabetically in sections indicating their area of specialization, such as 'Star and Feature', 'Musical', 'Comedians', 'Leading', 'Second Leading', 'Juvenile', 'Character', 'Trained Animals'. One category present in the first issue but no longer included was the 'Heavy Man', the villain in Victorian stock companies. Information supplied usually includes height, recent employment, dates and theatres played, and agents' addresses and telephone numbers.

Included in the 1952 edition of *The Spotlight* are the three artists opposite who have continued to pursue distinguished careers. In the 'Leading Man' section, Donald Sinden had already played Shakespearian and other major roles at Stratford, Bristol and London, as shown in the entry. The year was to signal an abrupt change of direction when he signed a film contract with the Rank Organisation, but he later returned to the stage, in characters ranging from Malvolio in *Twelfth Night* (1969), Sir Harcourt Courtly in *London Assurance* (1970), King Lear (1976), and Othello (1979), to twin roles in Terence Rattigan's double bill *In Praise of Love* (1973), and on television from *Our Man at St. Mark's* (1964) to *Two's Company* (1975).

Peter Barkworth, in the 'Juvenile-Character Men' section, a very young supporting actor in 1952, progressed to leading parts in the West End, including Edward VIII in *Crown Matrimonial* (1972), Headingly in *Donkeys' Years* (1976), and Philip Turner in *Can You Hear Me at the Back?* (1979). He also starred in the title role of the television series *Telford's Change* (1979).

Jane Asher is featured, aged six, in the children's section, with her younger sister Clare and brother Peter as 'The Asher Family' who 'All Have Red Hair'. She appeared as a child in numerous films, and plays, her adult roles including appearances in *Summer* (1968), *The Philanthropist* (1971), and as the Doctor, with Tom Conti, in *Whose Life is it Anyway?* (1978).

It is usual for an actor, when embarking on a career, to be seen by an agent while still at drama school, or while playing small parts with repertory companies. An agent may then sign up the artist on a percentage basis of any salary earned. This generally works well, as the agent may be able to negotiate a higher salary on behalf of his client, and is often contacted directly by managements, or film or television companies. *(JA)*

DONALD SINDEN

1952: The Brazilian in
"RED LETTER DAY"
—*Garrick Theatre*

1951: De Valreas in
"FROU-FROU"
—*Bernard Delfont Tour*

1950: BRISTOL OLD VIC

1949/50: Arthur Townsend in
"THE HEIRESS"
—*Haymarket Theatre*

1948: Sebastian in
"TWELFTH NIGHT"
—*Old Vic Company, New Theatre*

1946/47: STRATFORD-ON-AVON
FESTIVAL COMPANIES

Management:
FREDERICK

82

Height 5 feet 10¼ inches

PETER BARKWORTH

Charles Priest 1051

At present with
THE SHEFFIELD REPERTORY COMPANY
c/o "The Spotlight"

GERrard 3002

Alan Van Okker 1952

JANE ASHER
Nina in "MANDY" Ealing
SOPRANO

Casting: three artists from *The Spotlight Casting Directory*, No. 90 (July 1952)

This sketch-book is a unique document, created in unusual circumstances, of a remarkable production of Tchaikovsky's opera *The Queen of Spades* – the first in London since 1915, the first in English, and the first at Covent Garden. Forced to go to New York at a vital juncture in the run-up to the opening, the designer Oliver Messel (1905–1978) wrote a letter from New York to Michael Benthall, the director, in the form of this sketch-book. It gives detailed instructions and advice to those who had to translate his ideas into stage reality. Such details, seldom documented in this way, give a rare insight into a designer's imaginative processes.

It is clear from Messel's notes that because the opera had not been performed since 1915 there was little point in looking for precedents. He repeatedly urges Benthall to seek the advice of Lady Chilton, who had seen many performances in Imperial Russia and would be able to give first-hand information – even about 'the effective storm tricks' employed. Messel's references to source books for details of period rustic furniture and other items indicate his meticulous methods of working. His constant advice to consult the craftsmen involved – such as Jack Lovell, the property master – shows his close working relationship with them and his trust in their skill, even in his absence.

This sketch for Act III, Scene 1, 'The Barracks', in which Herman is haunted by visions of the dead Countess, shows Messel's method of creating and building atmosphere. As much attention is paid to sound and lighting as to the design: 'tap tap of stick and rustling of skirt . . . scattered leaves blow across the floor as door is blown open. Shadow creeps across floor and up the wall. Small section of window should open and blow the curtain out into the room.' Messel, dependant as he was on a third party to see his ideas realized, often refers in the letter to his assistant, Michael Northen, and reassures Michael Benthall that he can have complete confidence in him. It is interesting to note an unusual additional entry in the programme, 'Décor supervised by Michael Northen', since normally the designer alone gets a mention. *(JS)*

Sketch-book designs for *The Queen of Spades*
(Royal Opera House, Covent Garden, 1950)
Oliver Messel
Charcoal, pencil and ink 350 × 280
Michael Benthall Bequest [S.69–1976]

'This dress won't do. WSG. See over.' This curt comment was written by W. S. Gilbert (1836–1911) on the costume design (i, opposite) for Rudolph in *The Grand Duke*, submitted to him by Percy Anderson (1851–1928). Having recorded his disapproval, Gilbert turned Anderson's design over and drew exactly the costume he himself envisaged for the parsimonious Duke (ii, opposite), adding brief instructions to clarify the sketch: 'very rusty suit of black cloth – patched at the knees. Black cotton stockings, much darned – very dirty neck cloth and ruffles – any numbers of orders blazing on each breast. Collar of some order hanging around his shoulders (not shown in sketch). Ribbon across breast. General effect of extreme seediness relieved by numerous and brilliant decorations.'

Whether Anderson redesigned the costume in accordance with Gilbert's instructions is not known, but beyond doubt the photograph (iii, opposite) of Walter Passmore shows that he is wearing the costume that Gilbert commanded. These designs survive among a set of 79 that Percy Anderson made for the original production of *The Grand Duke*, and Gilbert's sketches and notes are so precise that the costumiers probably worked directly from them without further recourse to Anderson.

Gilbert always instructed his designers explicitly before they started work, having himself sketched the characters in his plot-books at a very early stage in the development of his script. A talented artist, Gilbert designed the costumes for several of the operas himself, and although many designers have found it restricting to work with an author-director who conceived the costumes so clearly, Anderson must have been used to Gilbert's dictatorial ways, having designed the costumes for the original productions of *The Yeomen of The Guard* (1888), *The Gondoliers* (1889), and *Utopia, Limited* (1893).

Gilbert's curt comment written on the design is characteristic of his uncompromising attitude when producing one of his own works. Nicknamed 'The Ironmaster at the Savoy', he knew every movement and grouping that he wanted from the start of the rehearsals – those for *The Grand Duke* being more gruelling than usual since he was suffering from gout. As Sullivan noted: 'Another week's rehearsal with WSG and I should have gone raving mad'.

The Grand Duke (7 March 1896) was the final opera in the series of thirteen that Gilbert wrote in collaboration with the composer Arthur Sullivan. Twenty-five years, many successes and a few disagreements separated this from the first opera, *Thespis*, and it seems that Gilbert's confidence in the popularity of the operas was waning by the 1890s, his insistence on spectacular sets and costumes for the last two operas perhaps reflecting an uncertainty that they were really worthy successors to such favourites as *The Mikado* (1885) and *The Gondoliers*. The costumes for *The Grand Duke* were, in the event, more highly praised in contemporary reviews than the opera itself. *(CH)*

iii **The finished costume.** Walter Passmore as Rudolph
in Act I of *The Grand Duke*
Cabinet photograph by Alfred Ellis
Given by Dame Bridget D'Oyly Carte

Very rusty suit of black cloth – patched at the knees
black cotton stockings, much darned – very dirty
wide cloth & ruffles – any number of orders blazing
on each breast – Collar of some order hanging round
his shoulders (not shown in sketch) Ribbon across
breast. General effect of extreme seediness relieved by
numerous & brilliant decoration.

i **Costume design** for Rudolph in Act I of *The Grand Duke*
(Savoy Theatre, London, 1896)
Percy Anderson
Pencil, watercolour, and bodycolour 228 × 135
Given by Dame Bridget D'Oyly Carte

ii **Costume design** for Rudolph in Act I of *The Grand Duke*
W. S. Gilbert
Pen and ink and pencil executed on the reverse of (i)
228 × 135
Given by Dame Bridget D'Oyly Carte

Buontalenti's *Il Giudizio di Paride (The Judgement of Paris)*, was a pastoral play performed as part of the wedding festivities of Prince Cosimo de' Medici and Maria Magdalena of Austria in 1608. The six acts were separated by *intermezzi* in which the scenic effects were far more spectacular than the setting for the play. This *intermezzo* by Strozzi celebrates the Florentine explorer Amerigo Vespucci (after whom the United States is named), and depicts his discovery of the West Indies.

In this natural setting by Giulio Parigi (1571–1635), a landscape draughtsman before his appointment as 'Architect and Engineer to the Medici' in 1606, a personified Tranquility is seated on the pinnacle of a coral-reef chariot, harnessed to two dolphins driven by Zephyrus, God of the West Wind. In addition, an actual figure from history, Vespucci, stands on the poop-deck of his ship. The different scenic effects would have followed one another in sequence, but the designer, traditionally, has amalgamated them in one image.

The great feature of these events was the changing of the various devices in full view of the audience, rather like the dissolve in a film sequence. The aim was to excite wonder and admiration at the ingenuity of the piece, brought off by the skill and craftsmanship of the engineers and backstage workers with highly complicated machinery. (An etching based on this drawing published by Parigi in the same year shows a cloud machine supporting Immortality and her celestial choir, together with Apollo and the Nine Muses.)

Three centuries later, in his production of Shakespeare's *Hamlet* for the Moscow Art Theatre in 1912, Edward Gordon Craig (1872–1966) designed a set also intended to change before the eyes of the audience. This was in direct opposition to the standard practice of the day, when illusion was preserved by the use of curtains to hide the scene-changes. Instead of elaborately painted flat scenes, Craig used undecorated screens, which, like the chariots and clouds of Parigi, were designed to turn and change by mechanical means. Craig gave their abstract form life and meaning by bathing the screens in coloured light.

Craig was obsessed with the role of Hamlet, having played the part himself, and still identifying closely with him – as demonstrated in the scene with his uncle, when he flooded the whole stage with gold light and dressed the screens and the actors in gold cloth, giving a sinister glint of corruption to the court. By contrast, the Players were dressed in clear bright colours, symbolizing, as Denis Bablet suggests, 'everything that was joyful'.

The screens were not actually used as Craig intended because technical difficulties made it necessary to change the screens behind curtains, destroying the effect he had desired. Nevertheless he introduced a new production concept whereby the setting as well as the action reflects the essence of the director's interpretation. *(JS)*

Model of a set for *Hamlet* (Moscow Art Theatre, 1912)
Edward Gordon Craig
Plaster 330 × 520 × 317
Given by the artist [E.2981–1934]

Design for the Fourth Intermezzo in *Il Giudizio di Paride*
(Uffizi Palace, Florence, 25 October 1608)
Giulio Parigi
Pen and ink 317 × 425 [S.295–1978]

Sophie Fedorovitch (1893–1953) is one of the most important contributors to the development of English stage design, particularly in the field of ballet. Frederick Ashton, for whom she designed eleven ballets of which *Nocturne* was one, thought she was the ideal designer for the dance because she liked to work closely with him, attending many rehearsals so that she could adapt her ideas to bring out the best in his choreography and in the dancer. Ashton found the simplicity of her approach reflected in the economy of means she used to create her costumes.

Fedorovitch appreciated that her designs should not impede the dancer or distract the audience. Her drawings were a point of departure rather than finished designs. She worked in the same way at costume fittings: only then would she determine the details, with great patience and exactness. Her method was a process of elimination, paring down the design until only the essential was left. Colour is a key factor, for she created subtle contrasts between strong and delicate shades to bring out the relationships of the dancers.

In the design opposite, the bright blue of the Reveller's costume contrasted with the soft greys worn by Margot Fonteyn in the leading part of the Poor Girl. Designers can draw attention in this way, either by subduing the leading costumes against a vibrant background, or by playing them up against a neutral one. With her suggestions of colour and delicate fabrics, Fedorovitch catches the nuances of mood and feeling created by the choreographer.

Fedorovitch's costumes thus express a theme rather than a character. The aim in designing costumes for a stage play such as *Arms and the Man* is rather to assist the actor in the portrayal of character. It is a more specific field of design, and requires greater precision of interpretation. Doris Zinkeisen (born in the early years of this century) displayed a flair for evoking period *pastiche* with wit and charm, and in Shaw's farce on the futility of war she emphasizes the bravura of the soldier Sergius by dressing him in a preposterous uniform combining the elements of chocolate-box Ruritanian elegance with that of the toy soldier.

The strutting, heel-clicking, moustache-twitching character was brilliantly portrayed by Laurence Olivier, critics describing him as 'the tinsel Prince' and referring to his 'Neapolitan ice-cream uniform'. This artful design shows all these elements in the choice of icing-sugar colours, the tinny nature of the decoration on the tunic, the exotic fur cap, and the almost childish rendering of the decorative embroidery on his breeches. The delicious costume must have played a part in Olivier's creation of a role in which it is said he was a 'museum of invention'. *(JS)*

Costume design for a Reveller in *Nocturne*
(Sadler's Wells Theatre, London, 1936)
Sophie Fedorovitch
Watercolour 401 × 259
Carr Doughty Collection [S.539–1980]

Costume design for Laurence Olivier as Sergius in
Arms and the Man (New Theatre, London, 1944)
Doris Zinkeisen
Pencil and watercolour 375 × 271 [S.185–1978]

'Whimsical Walker' (1850–1934) appeared in this clown's costume in a Royal Command Performance before Queen Victoria, a great circus lover, at Windsor Castle on 25 February 1886. The costume consists of a royal blue twill jacket *appliquéd* with the initials 'W.W', and pantaloons to match, both *appliquéd* with clown masks in 'suedette'.

Thomas Dawson Walker worked with most of the great circuses – Adams's in Yorkshire, Astley's, Hengler's, Barnum and Bailey's in America, Powell's and Clarke's – and performed principally with animals of all kinds. As a successful and much-loved clown in his thirties, he taught a donkey called Tom to sing to the accompaniment of toy bagpipes, a trombone, and a violin. The variation was necessary, because the donkey became bored by each instrument in turn, and was given encouragement by the next, until bribery in the shape of a sugar lump persuaded him to perform for his beloved master, on command, for the rest of his life.

The costumes worn by Whimsical Walker, who was a white-faced clown, were in the same tradition as those worn by the legendary Grimaldi (No. 24). (The other type of clown, the Auguste, of which Coco was an example, would wear a more outrageous make-up and outfit.) In his later years, as well as becoming one of the oldest active circus performers, Whimsical Walker appeared successfully as a straight actor on the stage and in numerous films.

The other costume shown opposite was worn by an unidentified actress playing the part of Principal Boy in a pantomime during the late nineteenth century. With its strong emphasis on the hips, the costume was designed by an unknown designer for an actress with opulent curves like those of Harriet Vernon –'a magnificent creature of ample figure', according to Augustus Harris – who took Principal Boy parts at Drury Lane in the 1880s.

The costume is similar in style to those designed by Charles Wilhelm and Percy Anderson for the Drury Lane pantomimes of that period, and has a crimson velvet cloak with a wide stand-up collar in the manner of a *Directoire* gentleman's coat collar, trimmed with black net over crimson satin, backed with crimson velvet. The net was hand-painted with gold metallic paint in a floral design, while the tight-waisted crimson satin tunic was embroidered with gold metallic braid, cord, and gold sequins, and decorated with gold thread and sequin tassels and bullion tassels of gold metallic thread. A pair of voluminous embroidered and decorated briefs matches the tunic. *(JA)*

Clown's costume worn by Whimsical Walker, 1886
Designer: unknown [S.279–1977]

Principal boy's costume from the 1880s
Designer: unknown
British Theatre Museum Association [1964/A51]

Ten years separate these designs, yet both reflect the revolution in British stage design which took place after the Second World War, first in opera, then in the theatre. Mussorgsky's *Boris Godunov* was Peter Brook's first production when in 1948 he was appointed director of productions of the Royal Opera House, Covent Garden, at the age of 22. While post-war austerity had created a nostalgia for the stereotyped grandeur characteristic of pre-war opera productions, Brook tried to relate the settings to the action in a more dramatic and imaginative way, retaining operatic grandeur but in a simplified form. He was greatly helped in this first effort by the inspired choice of the designer Georges Wakhevitch (b. 1907), whose Russian background brought a sympathetic approach both to the theme and to Brook's interpretation.

This can be seen clearly in Wakhevitch's design for Act I, Scene 2, which conjures up the atmosphere of a hideout in a poverty-stricken border town. The striped matting which draws the eye to the centre of the space leaps out of the sombre background of massive rough-hewn structures, whose abrasive surfaces of wood and stone create a kind of textural richness – as do the large props of crude earthenware and metal. This effect is softened to some extent by the red and yellow drapes, which lead in turn to the upper levels. The whole conception exactly matches the strength and simplicity of the music.

When Joan Littlewood established her Theatre Workshop at Stratford East in the mid-1950s, she too had to utilize scenic designers who could give imaginative expression to her revolutionary ideas. She was dissatisfied, like Peter Brook, with the technically smooth presentations of the West End, and suspicious of actors with preconceived techniques, tricks, and habits acquired over the years. She turned instead to actors from whose talent she could draw lively performances partly based on improvisation.

For Brendan Behan's play *The Hostage,* Joan Littlewood found in Sean Kenny (1932–1973) a designer who could realize her idea of a basic structure through and round which her actors could 'flow'. Kenny's architectural training ensured a down-to-earth, bare-bones approach. His sparse three-dimensional set allowed the actor that freedom so essential to Joan Littlewood's method of production. The set is permanent, with a central, semi-enclosed space serving as the doss-house-cum-brothel of the main action.

Like Wakhevitch in the previous design, Kenny makes use of the stage on several levels: some of the catwalks and platforms project into the acting area while others, intended for the song and dance routines that link the action, thrust out towards the audience. This submission of the sets to the action was a breakthrough after the imposed set-pieces of West End comedies. Although still confined within the proscenium arch it looked forward to a more three-dimensional, sculptural approach to stage design. *(JS)*

Set design for Act I, Scene 2, of *Boris Godunov*
(Royal Opera House, Covent Garden, 1948)
Georges Wakhevitch
Gouache 538 × 756
Arts Council Collection [S.854–1981]

Set design for *The Hostage*
(Theatre Royal, Stratford East, 1958)
Sean Kenny
Indian ink, felt pen, and crayon 250 × 355
British Council Collection [S.855–1981]

Only three years separate these designs by Erté and Fraser, and although their work appears very different in style, it reveals surprising similarities. Both men loved the fantastic and the dramatic; both concentrated on shape, working often with pen and ink to delineate sharp outline and fine detail; and both had expert practical knowledge of costume-making for the realization of their designs.

Erté was born Romain de Tirtoff in St. Petersburg in 1892, and created his name from the French pronunciation of his initials 'RT'. The stage was an ideal home for his lively decorative style and his love of flamboyant colours, and his theatrical work flourished alongside his fashion career. One of the extravagant costumes which he created for himself to wear at masked balls 'was inspired by the imaginary Orient; it was very tight-fitting, in silver *lamé*, with many strings of pearls which ran from the legs to the arms'. In this, it was similar to the design reproduced opposite for the almost hermaphrodite Prince costume, bedecked with the strings of pearls that Erté loved and saw as living objects when the dancer was in motion.

Trained as a painter in oils, Erté used *gouache* for his theatrical designs, and here the thick droplets of white *gouache* used for the pearls make them stand out in relief, contrasting with the flat gold of the trousers decorated with blood-red pendant jewels. Other touches of colour create a startling effect: the sapphire in the head-dress, the gold finger-rings, the scarlet lipstick, the blue eyes, and the scarlet and orange curls from the end of the head-dress. Brightly coloured curls also come in from the right of the design enhancing its serpentine, lambent quality.

Unlike Erté's long career, that of Claud Lovat Fraser was tragically short. Born in 1890, he died at the age of 31 having established himself as a leading graphic artist and theatrical designer. Taught to paint in oils at art school, he preferred to work with reed and mapping pens and watercolour, a medium which suited his precise style perfectly. Perhaps his best known theatrical designs were those for the set and costumes of John Gay's *The Beggar's Opera*, directed by Nigel Playfair at the Lyric Theatre, Hammersmith, in June 1920, and in the finished design for the earthy character Lockit illustrated opposite, the deft pen delineations of Lockit's features reveal mastery of caricature. Fraser's designs captured the essence of the characters as well as the basic 'lines' and colours they should wear. Lockit's coat is blue; his waistcoat a muddy yellow; he carries an orange kerchief and the heels of his shoes are a surprisingly dashing red.

For all his stage designs Fraser produced clear line working-drawings, with samples of material attached and detailed instructions to the costumiers. Finished designs, such as this for Lockit, were made after the working-drawings. Fraser supervised the costume-making on this production, and insisted that the beggars' disreputable clothes should first be made perfectly as new, then torn and splashed with dirty paint water to achieve the correct effect. *(CH)*

Costume design for Prince Assad in 'Dance de Fouet',
from the revue *A Thousand and One Nights* (Bataclan
Theatre, Paris, 1917)
Erté (pseudonym of Romain de Tirtoff)
Pen, ink, watercolour, and gouache 238 × 150
Circ. 981–1967
© Sevenarts Ltd.

Costume design for Arthur Wynn as Lockit in *The
Beggar's Opera* (Lyric Theatre, Hammersmith, 1920)
Claud Lovat Fraser
Pen, ink, and watercolour 191 × 106
Circ. 312–1928

Detailed, historically accurate costume designs were much in demand for late nineteenth- and early twentieth-century productions, in France as well as in England. This design for Debussy's opera *Pelléas et Mélisande*, based on a play by Maeterlinck, shows how the designer Charles Bianchini (1860–1905) executed his commission in a manner typical of many costume designers of his day, leaving few details of the costume open to interpretation.

Costume design, albeit of flamboyant stylized rococo clothes, played a much more important part in French theatre of the eighteenth century than in England, where actresses wore the most fashionable clothes or donned approximations of 'eastern' or 'classical' clothes if the play demanded. In France, the authors Voltaire and Diderot advocated the reform of stage costuming, and the actor Talma took the innovative step of appearing in Voltaire's *Brutus* (1789) in authentic Roman costume, copied by the painter David from a Roman statue. Important developments were also made by Paul Lormier, a designer at the Paris Opéra in the 1840s and 1850s, whose efforts to produce accurate costumes through historical research were paralleled in England by the work undertaken by Charles Kean for his productions in the 1850s.

Despite mixed critical reaction to the music of Debussy's opera *Pelléas and Mélisande*, Bianchini's costumes were much admired. Through reference to books on medieval dress, Bianchini drew a meticulous design for Mélisande's costume, noting in the top right-hand corner: 'Mélisande 3e tableau 4e tableau puis tête nue' (Mélisande 3rd scene, 4th scene then bare-headed'). The design is lean and elegant, with an emphasis on sinuous line common to many French designers and *couturiers*. Colour is only indicated by emerald green on the sleeve quatrefoils, head-dress, and jewel decoration on the bodice. An inset detail shows the basic shape for the jewel, and a note has been added on the material to be used for the dress –'crêpe chine' (chinese silk).

Mary Garden was the singer who originally created the role of Mélisande. Another note, deleted in pencil, refers to the impracticability of the length of material from the medieval head-dress designed to continue under the chin: 'elle ne mettra jamais la mentonette' ('she will never wear the chin strap'). So, in the finished costume, the restricting veil under the singer's chin has been dispensed with, and strict historical accuracy sacrificed to practical necessity.

The pearls which Bianchini showed on the sleeve are repeated as hair decoration, and the sleeve itself continues further over the hand. The pendant veils hanging from the bands of material on the upper arm have been extended to floor length, and a long train added. The costumier interpreted the intricate pattern on the dress by either *appliqué* or embroidery, and, despite alterations, the finished costume remained true to the original conception and spirit of Bianchini's design. *(CH)*

Costume design for Mary Garden as Mélisande in
Pelléas et Mélisande (Opéra-Comique, Paris, 1902)
Charles Bianchini
Pen, pencil, and ink 313 × 241 [S.161–1977]

Mary Garden in the finished costume, 1902,
from *L'Art du Théâtre*, No. 20 (1902)

Andrew Lloyd Webber, who composed the music for *Jesus Christ Superstar*, regarded the show as an experiment to see whether he and Tim Rice, the lyricist, could write a popular piece that was all music, and no dialogue. To portray Jesus on stage as a pop star was a daring idea which required sensitivity and understanding from everyone involved: what emerged was a rock opera akin to a cartoon version of the gospel, set in the week before the crucifixion. Paul Nicholas, with a trim beard and white robe, was the first angry young Jesus, with an appropriately moody pop-star quality, singing vigorously and boiling with an energy and enthusiasm which grabbed the audience.

The robe shown here, designed by Gabriella Falk, is of ankle-length rayon linen weave, with silk fringe at the bottom edge, and long sleeves. The crown of thorns consists of a frame of mild steel wire lapped with leather. Fastened to the frame with steel wire are polythene trellis strips with aluminium paint. The traditional style of Jesus's robe created an almost timeless effect through its contrast with the contemporary costume of the other characters – such as the apostles' women, who wore sleeveless low-necked teeshirts and jeans, or slim-fitting tunic tops and *culottes*. The longest running musical in British theatre history to date, *Jesus Christ Superstar* experienced, in Elizabeth Grice's phrase, 3,357 resurrections.

Though the glitter sometimes outweighs the gold in Elton John's music, he has always been a consummate performer. From the moment he appeared on stage at Los Angeles's Troubadour Club in August 1970, dressed in yellow Mr. Freedom overalls, a Donald Duck bib, and aluminium-painted boots to perform in a concert that stunned the audience with both its emotional range and its athletic prowess (including press-ups on the piano), he has never ceased to exploit extravagant theatre. Perhaps John's crucial importance is that he showed that not all successful singer/composers need cultivate their egos through sententiousness and bombast. In spite of the fact that John's synthesis of hard-rock piano, lush orchestration, and impeccable production are sometimes wasted on the mawkish and rambling, he has constantly produced polished pop. This, allied with his love of live performance, his fairy-tale career story, and his enormous income, has enabled him to retain his sense of delight.

The costume opposite, known as 'Bicycle John', was designed by Bill Whitten. The tunic-style jacket is in striped pink, orange, silver, green, red, and purple lurex. A bicycle bell is at the centre edge of the tunic, chromium-plated bicycle mudguards form the epaulets, while bicycle reflectors decorate the skin-tight jeans, which are made of black lurex. Knee-high black leather boots, with platform soles and four-inch heels covered in multi-coloured sequins, complete the outfit. *(JA/DF)*

Costume worn by Paul Nicholas as Jesus in *Jesus Christ Superstar* (Palace Theatre, London, 1972)
Designer: Gabriella Falk
Given by the Robert Stigwood Organisation
S.104A–1981

'Bicycle John' costume worn by Elton John
(US tour, 1974–75)
Designer: Bill Whitten
Given by Elton John [S.233–1977]

Abstract painters of the 1930s found an extension of their art in designing for the stage. The three-dimensional nature of stage presentation enabled them to experiment with dramatic contrasts of curved shapes and areas of flat brilliant colour. The great interest of Léger (1881–1955) in machines led him to dehumanize the human body in his paintings and to create ballet designs in which the dancers appeared as a mobile part of the décor. This merging of the dancer with the scenery may have influenced Lifar's choice of Léger to design the sets and costumes for *David triomphant*.

As *maître de ballet* and premier *danseur* at the Paris Opéra, Serge Lifar wished to restore the reputation of the ballet in France, and *David triomphant* was one of several biblical and classical themes he used to exalt the heroic male character. As leading solo male dancer and choreographer, he created for himself a series of strong, slow movements based on those of classical ballet, but emphasizing their architectural and monumental shape.

Léger's design expresses this monumental quality. The square panels of bold, primitive colour and barbaric costumes make a vibrant contrast with the smooth, rounded columns and straight lines of the stairs and throne, and create their own tension, life, and rhythm. Lifar had strong views about the rhythmic qualities of dance, believing that it had its own inherent music and did not need the support of orchestrated sound. He used rhythms which emanated from dance itself, such as tapping feet and the rhythmic beats and swings produced by the human body in movement.

The involvement of John Piper (b. 1903) with the abstractionists was fairly shortlived, and came at a period of uncertainty in his development as a painter. The Group Theatre was a private experimental theatre society founded in 1933 by Stephen Spender, W. H. Auden, and Christopher Isherwood. In 1938 it produced Spender's play *Trial of a Judge*, dealing with the extremes of communism and fascism, at Unity Theatre, a politically-oriented theatre club: 'art politics' were not in Piper's nature, but his admiration for Spender as a poet and the potential for abstraction in stage design probably attracted him to the project.

Piper's use of large areas of the cool tones of blue, grey, and black show an English restraint, while the warmer yellows and reds which dominate Léger's design suggest the latter's European background and the influence of Italian primitives. With his designs for *Trial of a Judge*, Piper felt he had plunged head-first into a fascinating new art form. It was an important turning point in his artistic development, for in taking this step he realized the fallacy of the abstractionists' denial of a national style and grew more confident in expressing ideas according to his own nature. Since then he has produced much stage design with an unmistakably English flavour and setting, notably for the premieres of Benjamin Britten's operas, *Billy Budd* (1951) and *The Turn of the Screw* (1954). *(JS)*

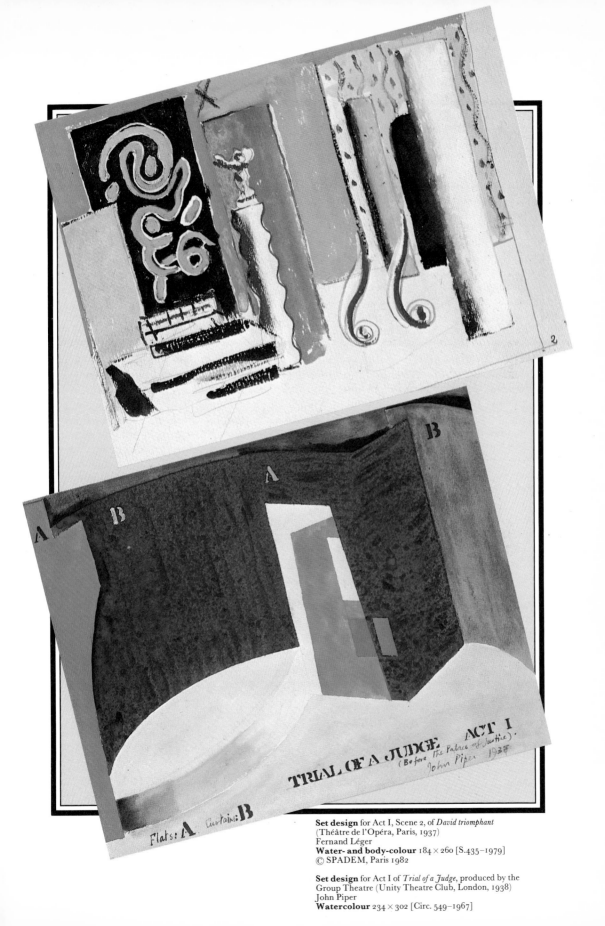

Set design for Act I, Scene 2, of *David triomphant*
(Théâtre de l'Opéra, Paris, 1937)
Fernand Léger
Water- and body-colour 184 × 260 [S.435–1979]
© SPADEM, Paris 1982

Set design for Act I of *Trial of a Judge*, produced by the
Group Theatre (Unity Theatre Club, London, 1938)
John Piper
Watercolour 234 × 302 [Circ. 549–1967]

Across 250 years, these two costumes show how costume designs have evolved from those tailored to the human form, as in the early eighteenth-century Italian costume, to the ultra-modernity of Alwin Nikolais's tubular style, which completely disguises the dancer's body and turns the human frame into an abstract form. The contrast demonstrates, too, how dance has become a form in itself.

The rose-coloured velvet costume is a very early surviving example of costumes made specifically for the stage, and was used for plays by Goldoni and for masques and other courtly entertainments in which dancing was an important element. It is one of twenty-three similar costumes in the Theatre Museum and comes from the private theatre built in 1741 in the Castle of Meleto in Tuscany.

The cut of the costume and the style of the embroidery probably date from the early eighteenth century. The costume consists of a coarse hessian base laced down the back by means of eyelet holes. It is overlaid with velvet, and decorated with raised silver embroidery in purl and thread in a stylized design of flowers and scrolls on the body, with individual motifs on the *peplum*, or skirt. Two velvets of the late seventeenth century have been used – the second, just visible at the centre of the *peplum*, has been re-used to repair the first. Furnishing velvet rather than finger velvet was used as being more effective in candlelight and because it would better withstand the weight of the metallic embroidery. The use of such precious metals and expensive fabrics was only within the means of rich aristocrats.

The second costume was designed by Alwin Nikolais for 'Finials', a section of his *Allegory*, first produced on 30 January 1959. Nikolais was responsible for the choreography, costumes, sound, and lighting. The costume, which completely encased the dancer, is of yellow wool jersey over a frame of separate wire hoops; the hips and knees are suggested at appropriate points, and there is a detachable head-piece. As C. Ray Smith observes generally of Nikolais's costumes, the effect is such that 'the dancers themselves are ambiguously dematerialized and fuse with both costumes and sets into a unified revelation that is inexplicably thrilling'.

Dancer, choreographer, author, teacher, and ballet director, Nikolais, born in Connecticut in 1912, was a puppet-master early in his career, before he eventually became the foremost dance innovator of the 1960s. His choreography has an innate source of energy which gives animation to abstract forms, patterns, colours, and sounds; he also supervises every aspect of each production he undertakes. *(JA)*

Italian eighteenth-century stage costume
Designer: unknown [S.92–1978]

Dance costume from 'Finials', a section of *Allegory*
(Henry Street Playhouse, New York, 1959
Designer: Alwin Nikolais
Given by the designer [S.455–1979]

The reputation of Philip James de Loutherbourg (1740–1812) had preceded his arrival in England in 1771, when David Garrick engaged him as 'Superintendent of Scenery and Machinery' at Drury Lane. After ten years there he left to work on his 'Eidophusikon', a three-dimensional panoramic device for public exhibition based on his method of preparing small-scale models of his stage designs, but in 1785 he made a brief but flamboyant come-back to the theatre with the Covent Garden pantomime *Omai; or, A Trip Round the World*. For this, his designs were inspired by sketches of Cook's voyages published during 1782–84. The model opposite has been variously ascribed to *Omai* and to an earlier pantomime, *Robinson Crusoe* (1781), but, since it does not tally very satisfactorily with the description of the scenes in either work, its identity remains uncertain.

De Loutherbourg's skill is evident in his application of techniques he introduced to England from the Continent. He cleverly represents large masses in the sheer rock faces, and breaks up the central space with ground-rows and cut-outs in the form of rocky outcrops, huts, ship's tackle, and a small boat. He also devised sophisticated lighting effects at Drury Lane. By placing pivoting coloured silk screens in front of wing- and backlights, he could suddenly vary their colour and intensity to create atmosphere.

De Loutherbourg's elaborate perspective scenery was meant to be seen through the frame of a proscenium arch, unlike the designs of Roger Butlin (b. 1935) for Euripides's *Medea*, prepared in this model for Greenwich Theatre, which has no proscenium, wings, or flies, and an acting area which consists of an apse-shaped space and a thrust stage. The steeply-raked auditorium allows the total height of the 35-foot back wall to be seen from every seat in the house, and the closeness of the audience to the stage makes it impossible to create illusionist scenery. Butlin's approach was thus sculptural, relying on imagery and texture to make an impact on the audience.

In *Medea*, a fan of radiating steel rods, spreadeagled like the wings of a bird, transforms into the sun-chariot in which Medea makes her escape. This three-dimensional structure combines its aerial quality with rigid strength as it thrusts up from the flat surface of the sandy floor, representing a sun-scorched desert. It provides a pivot for the action, through and round which the actors can move freely. Although Butlin's set may seem to offer 'a meagre diet of visual nourishment' as one critic suggested, this is not the result of economic necessity, but a conscious attempt to break away from pictorial representation. *(JS)*

Model of quay and beach setting, between 1771 and 1785
Philip James de Loutherbourg
Watercolour and varnish 531 × 787 × 457 [E.161–1937]

Model for set for *Medea* (Greenwich Theatre, 1970)
Roger Butlin
Mixed media 327 × 610 × 479
Arts Council Collection [S.472–1980]

The immense success of Diaghilev's oriental ballet *Schéhérazade* in 1910 led him to embark on another, this time with an Indo-Siamese background based on a Hindu legend. The idea for *Le Dieu bleu* was suggested by Fokine, who had been impressed by the Bangkok Royal Ballet dancers he had seen at St. Petersburg in 1900. Although the ballet was not successful ultimately, and only remained in the repertoire for one year, the fact that it followed *Schéhérazade* meant that it had to exceed it in sumptuousness and fantasy. Bakst (1866–1924), now at the height of his powers, excelled himself in his interpretation of the theme.

This design for Young Rajahs was probably unrealized, since no such characters are mentioned in the programme, but it demonstrates the incredible richness of the production, as Richard Buckle describes it: 'there has never been such an elaboration of gold and pearl embroidery, such luxuriously twined and dizzily towering turbans, hung with such yards of pleated gauze or festooned with such swags of beads'.

Bakst's bold yet subtle use of colour was one of the hallmarks of his genius. He held that 'in each colour of the prism there exists a gradation which sometimes expresses frankness and chastity, sometimes sensuality and even bestiality, sometimes pride, sometimes despair. This can be felt and given over to the public by the effect one makes of the various shadings. That is what I tried to do in *Schéhérazade*. Against a lugubrious green I put a blue full of despair, paradoxical as it may seem. There are reds which are triumphal and there are reds which assassinate. . . . The painter who knows how to make use of this . . . can draw from the spectator the exact emotion which he wants them to feel' (as quoted in C. Spencer, *Bakst*, 1971).

It is by this orchestration of colour that Bakst attacks our senses. Here, his use of a warm, deep yellow for the main part of the robe (probably to be interpreted as a rich silk brocade), patterned with elaborate cartouches of dark blue, conjures up the hot exotic climate of the Orient. This is balanced by touches of blue and citrus yellow, interspersed with areas of brilliant white which cleverly neutralize the clash of yellows. The whole effect characterizes the gaudy yet dignified appearance of the rajahs.

Perhaps Diaghilev's wish to outdo *Schéhérazade* caused *Le Dieu bleu* to fail, and the sight of Nijinsky as the god, decorated from head to foot in 'deep azure blue' greasepaint, was too much for the public to take seriously. This production marked the end of Diaghilev's preoccupation with exoticism. He realized that this style was being overtaken by the modernists and turned his attention to wooing such artists as Picasso, Braque, and de Chirico to design for him. *(JS)*

Costume design for 'Young Rajahs' in *Le Dieu bleu*
(Théâtre du Châtelet, Paris, 1912)
Léon Bakst
Pencil and watercolour 285 × 207 [S.338–1981]

After the scene-painter John Grieve started work at Covent Garden in 1806, and was joined by his sons, Thomas in 1817 and William in 1819, the family team dominated scenic production there until 1835, when they moved to Drury Lane. William died in 1844 and his father in 1845, but Thomas carried on until his death in 1882, working for Charles Kean at the Princess's Theatre during the 1850s, assisted in later years by his son, Thomas Walford Grieve.

The Grieves either used the traditional arrangement of drops or flats with regularly spaced wings, or set scenes introduced to England by de Loutherbourg (see No. 65), which used diagonally placed groundrows and cut-outs to break up the stage space. Although the Grieves devoted themselves exclusively to the theatre, unlike their contemporary Clarkson Stanfield (who practised both easel art and scene-painting), they too 'painted pictures'. William Grieve's design for Act III, Scene 2, of an adaptation of Rossini's opera *The Siege of Corinth*, 'Ruins of the Temple of Neptune with the Acro-Corinthus in the distance', was singled out for special praise, and its title gives a clue to the development of scene painting at the time.

The expansion of foreign travel and the practice of sending artists abroad to record expeditions aroused great interest in exotic places, and created a fashion for ancient and classical stories. Such subjects could be exploited in the theatre with spectacular scenes designed to be as architecturally accurate as possible. Archaeological accuracy was also striven for, especially after 1823 when J. R. Planché set a new standard of antiquarian accuracy in Charles Kemble's production of *King John*.

The cause of realism was furthered by the Grieves' invention of moving panoramic views, and the appetite for spectacular presentation found extravagant expression in Augustus Harris's annual Christmas pantomimes at Drury Lane, the choice for 1889 being *Jack and the Beanstalk*. Immense sums were lavished on the costumes, designed by Wilhelm, and on the scenery, and the music hall star Dan Leno was engaged to play the Dame.

As was customary, a team of designers, which included Robert Caney, painted the scenes. The programme credits him with Scenes VI and XII, but he probably assisted with others. For Scene VI, 'Mrs Simpson's Back Garden', he created a charmingly realistic backyard with ramshackle outhouses and seasonal fat turkeys in the background, the whole scene being dominated by the huge beanstalk in the centre. According to *The Daily Telegraph*, the stalk rose to the heavens via the roof-tops – also beautifully captured by Caney in a scene-change – to the 'Giant's Castle in Cloudland', eventually reaching Mount Olympus. The traditional introduction of acrobats and jugglers into the story was cleverly handled in this production when Carl Abbs, the 'Strong Man', gave his performance from the topmost branches of the beanstalk. *(JS)*

Set design for Act III, Scene 2, of *The Siege of Corinth*
(Theatre Royal, Drury Lane, 1836) William Grieve
Pen and ink and watercolour 190 × 302
Gabrielle Enthoven Collection, given by John W. Grieve
[S.858–1981]

Set design for Scene VI of *Jack and the Beanstalk*
(Theatre Royal, Drury Lane, 1889) Robert Caney
Pen and ink and watercolour 198 × 270
Gabrielle Enthoven Collection [S.864–1981]

The Graecian-style costume worn by Lillah McCarthy as Helena in Harley Granville-Barker's production of *A Midsummer Night's Dream* at the Savoy Theatre, 6 February 1914, was designed by Norman Wilkinson of Four Oaks (1882–1934), one of several artists, including Albert Rutherston and Charles Ricketts, whom Granville-Barker brought in from outside the theatre to design his productions. The costume is made of ivory silk, decorated with a cyclamen-pink stencilled floral design. Over the dress is a tunic in the same colour and style, edged with silk macramé fringe with silver thread circular tassels and red beads. The tunic has a cord belt of silver thread edged with silver thread circular tassels. The dress was worn with mauve shoes and a fair wig, according to the description in the production Accounts Book held by the British Theatre Association.

Wilkinson deliberately (and controversially) designed relatively simple settings in an incongruous mixture of styles to suggest the mortal and immortal worlds. The costume harmonized with the stylized Greek settings of the Athenian scenes, which reflected the tangible world of the mortals: their palace was a solid structure of black and gold, in direct contrast to the unreal world of the fairies, who had gold faces and hands with costumes of gold and silver to make them seem 'remote from humanity', as Gordon Marshall observed. They appeared against a woodland background which consisted simply of curtains lit in changing tones of green, blue, and violet.

The Astrologer's costume was worn by the Swiss high-tenor Hugues Cuenod in Robert Helpmann's production of Rimsky-Korsakov's opera *Le Coq d'or*, completed in 1907, first staged in Moscow in 1909, and receiving only its second British production at Covent Garden, on 7 January 1954. The Astrologer is a narrator figure who presents the fairy-tale world of King Dodon to the audience, and this costume, designed by Loudon Sainthill (1919–1969) who also did the settings, captures the element of fantasy. It is in bottle-green velvet, *appliquéd* with designs of the sun's rays in yellow felt, and has tight-fitting full-length saxe blue velvet sleeves with bottle-green felt cuffs. Strips of pleated navy blue nylon are draped from each shoulder, while ribbons of multi-coloured cotton braid hang from the back of the left sleeve. The skirt is of hand-painted velvet in a design representing the sun's rays and clouds in shaded greens and blues, *appliquéd* with felt stars sprayed with gold paint. *(JA)*

Costume worn by Lillah McCarthy as Helena in
A Midsummer Night's Dream (Savoy Theatre, London,
1914)
Designer: Norman Wilkinson of Four Oaks
British Theatre Museum Association. 1966/A/216

Costume worn by Hugues Cuenod as the Astrologer in
Le Coq d'or (Royal Opera House, Covent Garden, 1954)
Designer: Loudon Sainthill [S.33–1980]

Diaghilev's celebrated ballet company presented the first performance of the ballet *Barabau* at the London Coliseum on 11 December 1925. Choreographed by the young George Balanchine, who had joined the company the previous year, the ballet was inspired by an Italian nursery rhyme and set in a village in northern Italy. Diaghilev had met the composer, Vittorio Rieti, in Venice that summer, and being unable to find a prestigious Italian artist to design the scenery and costumes, Diaghilev decided to go to the famous painter of Montmartre street scenes, Maurice Utrillo.

This pencil sketch, marked on a grid from nought to twelve, was executed by Diaghilev's talented scene-painter, Prince Schervashidze, copying from an original design by Utrillo. For this purpose, Schervashidze ignored the fine details that Utrillo always included, concentrating instead on the proportions. He measured and enlarged the church doorway and arch to make entries practical, then trimmed the sketch to plan further enlargements that he executed directly on the cloth. At that point he painted the details of the village, and reproduced only the central part of the design, eliminating part of the trees on the right-hand side and the building on the extreme left.

The prolific Maurice Utrillo (1883–1955) was living at the Château de Saint-Bernard, near Lyons, when Diaghilev's 'secretary', Boris Kochno, visited him. He sat in silence throughout the meeting, asking nothing about the ballet. 'It was enough for him to know that he was being asked to paint "a landscape with a church" and no further details seemed to interest him', wrote Kochno. This was not surprising, since by 1925 Utrillo had been committed to lunatic asylums eight times, and had been a confirmed alcoholic since the age of thirteen.

By 1924 Utrillo was a celebrity, his paintings sought by every dealer in Paris, and yet, caring for nothing but alcohol, painting, and toys, all his affairs were managed by Utter who called him 'the best business proposition of the century'. Utrillo's mother had taught him to paint as therapy when it had become evident that he could never hold down a job, and the painting of street scenes obsessed him. Figures were rarely included in his painting, but when forced to sketch some costume designs for *Barabau* they were the clothes of the figures that sometimes peopled his works. The church for the backcloth was that of Saint-Bernard in the village near the Château, possibly painted from postcards. As one acquaintance noted: 'His mind consists of churches, houses, and streets. Isn't that enough?'. *(CH)*

Backcloth for *Barabau* (London Coliseum, 1925)
Prince Schervashidze after Maurice Utrillo
Peinture à la détrempe on canvas 10,320 × 12,300
Presented by the Friends of the Museum of Performing
Arts and acquired by them with a generous donation from
Lord Grade [S.454–1980]

Working sketch for backcloth for *Barabau*
(London Coliseum, 1925)
Prince Schervashidze after Maurice Utrillo
Pencil 165 × 260 [S.186–1978]

There are two basic methods of painting scenic cloths, whether for 'flown' or built scenery. The 'English' way is illustrated by Joseph Harker at work in his South London studio on a panoramic backcloth for the 1914 Covent Garden production of *Parsifal*. The canvas is nailed out on a vertical frame, which can be winched up or down to the required working height. Space is needed below floor level to enable the frame to be dropped through and then gradually pulled up, and a high roof is necessary to expose the whole cloth. (In the paintshop of the National Theatre, London, a moveable lift is used to reach the working area.)

Alternatively, there is the 'continental' method, which is to paint the cloth horizontally on the floor, as is here happening to Oliver Messel's backcloth for *The Sleeping Beauty* production of 1946, in process of being painted on the Covent Garden stage. This method requires a level, smooth surface with enough room to walk around the stretched cloth, and good overhead lighting.

In both cases the fire-proofed cloths – usually canvas, although hessian or gauze can be used – have to be prepared for painting. 'Continental' cloths are treated with fine French glue, while 'English' cloths used to be treated on the frame with a heavy molten size. Unfortunately, this made the thick paint on top liable to crack, and the completed cloths became impractical to fold for storage and transport. This limitation has now been overcome by the use of a thin emulsion medium mixed with whiting, which also allows for a much wider variety of painting techniques to be used, such as dyeing directly into the cloth, and thin, 'watercolour' effects.

Once the cloth has been primed, it is squared-up to correspond to the designer's sketch, and the design is then sketched on to the cloth with a piece of charcoal set in a long holder. The paint – powder pigment mixed with water and medium or size – is meanwhile prepared in buckets or tins and heated as necessary if size is being used. It is applied by brush, generally starting at the top if the cloth is vertical, or from the middle outwards when on the floor. Other techniques such as spraying, stencilling, and sponge-ing can also be used. *(AT)*

Painting a backcloth for Act III of the Sadler's Wells
Ballet production of *The Sleeping Beauty* (1946) on the stage
at Covent Garden
Photograph by Edward Mandinian

Scene Painting
Joseph Harker working on a backcloth for the 1914 Covent
Garden production of *Parsifal*.
From a reproduction in *The Illustrated London News*,
31 January 1914
Frédéric de Haenen
Sheet cut to 366 × 230
Gabrielle Enthoven Collection

As in so many aspects of theatre work, the creation of costumes is a combined effort, in this case involving the collaboration of the designer and the costumier whose mutual understanding and readiness to reach a compromise is vital to the finished product. In the first illustration here, Oliver Messel, on leave from war service in 1942, is with Matilda Etches in her studio discussing his sketches for Helpmann's ballet after *Comus*, surrounded by the fabrics to be used.

The term to 'build' a costume is very expressive of the process involved, for as another costume designer, Edmund Brady, has said, 'costumes must be as durable as combat uniforms'. The choice of fabric depends as much on the stresses and strains it will have to endure as on imaginative decisions about colour and texture, and this is particularly true of dancers' costumes, where constant movement and stretching puts extra strain on the material. Look inside a theatrical costume – no matter how diaphanous – and you will be amazed at the tough lining, strong double stitching, and heavy-duty clasps, zips and press-studs. However right the costume appears on stage, it is absolutely essential that the dancer feels secure and unselfconscious in it.

The designer will usually have firm ideas as to the colour combinations required. The costumier will advise on the best fabrics which may have to be specially dyed to match – bearing in mind cut, durability, how they will move, and how they will behave under artificial light. Each brings his or her own expertise to bear on the practical problem of translating the design into a working costume.

The dress form in the background is an indispensable aid to the costumier. Adjusted to the exact measurements of the dancer, it acts not only as a substitute for the absent performer but also supports the garment, which can sometimes become surprisingly heavy, and makes working on the costume easier during construction.

The question of movement is all-important in the choice and cut of cloth for dancers. Not all fabrics flow or move well when cut, to create the right line during the course of the dance. Our stage-two illustration of Miss Etches, this time with Sophie Fedorovitch and Palma Nye for de Valois's ballet *Orpheus and Eurydice*, demonstrates the priority given to this aspect of movement. This in turn will affect the play of light on the surface, perhaps changing the total quality of the colour.

In the final stage, costume and dancer come together for one of the last fittings, when adjustment to details such as cuffs is more significant. A fitting might take place after a dress rehearsal, when the costume is seen for the first time under the conditions in which it will appear. Some decoration, although attractive in itself, may not read well from a distance or be 'washed out' by the lighting. In most cases details are removed rather than added. *(JS)*

The Costumier: Matilda Etches
i with Oliver Messel discussing his designs for *Comus*
(New Theatre, London, 1942)
Photograph by Germaine Kanova

iii with Oliver Messel and an assistant checking details of
Margot Fonteyn's costume for *Comus*, 1942
Photograph by Germaine Kanova

ii with Sophie Fedorovitch watching Palma Nye testing the
cut of her costume for *Orpheus and Eurydice*
(New Theatre, London, 1941)
Photograph by 'Anthony'

The term properties (or 'props') in the theatre refers to any article used during a performance which does not come under the heading of costume, furniture, or scenery – though sometimes it is difficult to distinguish props from items of costume. Mistinguett's pink ostrich feather fan, which was a decorative part of her costume, was also functional, since it nearly succeeded in camouflaging her from the eyes of three-quarters of the crowned heads of Europe. The 'Excalibur' sword, designed by Edward Burne-Jones (1833–1898) and used by Henry Irving in the title role of *King Arthur* in 1895, was conceived as part of the whole production: its metal scabbard has the Knights of the Round Table modelled in bas-relief and is painted with decorated motifs.

An early example of a practical 'trick' prop is David Garrick's dagger, *c.* 1750, which has a retractable blade. Personal props such as these are entrusted to the performers, but checked by the stage manager before the performance. In most cases, however, the stage manager has direct responsibility for all props, and checks that they are set correctly on stage. Props which have to be brought on by an actor are arranged on a table backstage and usually handed to him by an assistant stage manager, who relieves him of them on his exit.

Props may be straightforward items such as the zither, the painted wood truncheon, or Yorick's skull (made of polyester resin and earth), or they can be more elaborate affairs. Oscar Asche, who produced his own record-breaking play *Chu-Chin-Chow* (which ran at His Majesty's Theatre from 1916 to 1922), employed a Wedgwood potter who sat on stage making earthenware pots. The one shown is signed by Oscar Asche and his wife Lily Brayton, and dated 1916–17–18–19. A striking feature of the Les Paul guitar used by Pete Townshend of The Who, *c.* 1969, is that it was intended for use at one performance only: it served in the combined role of musical instrument and prop, since it was purposely broken at a performance. *(JA)*

Properties (see opposite).

Foreground, left to right:
Skull. Used in *Hamlet* (National Theatre, London, 1976)
Polyester resin with earth
Given by the Governors of the National Theatre.
S.792–1981

Dagger with retractable blade. Used by David Garrick
in stage performance, *c.* 1750
**Steel with hilt covered in blue shagreen, decorated
with silver braid**
British Theatre Museum Association, given by
Stafford Byrne [1963/G/147]

Truncheon. Used by Rutland Barrington in *The Pirates of
Penzance* (Opéra Comique, London, 1880)
Painted wood
Given by Dame Bridget D'Oyly Carte

Sword. Used by Henry Irving in *King Arthur* (Lyceum
Theatre, London, 1895)
Various metals and paint
British Theatre Museum Association:
The Irving Archive [1963/G/61]

Middleground, left to right:
Zither. Used by Beatrice Lillie in *An Evening with Beatrice
Lillie* (Globe Theatre, London, 1954)
Painted lacquer
Given by Beatrice Lillie [S.330–1979]

Flowers. Used by Alicia Markova in *Giselle*, Vic-Wells
Ballet (now the Royal Ballet), 1934
Silver foil
Cyril Beaumont Collection [S.262, 263–1979]

Stage jewellery. Used by Madame Vestris, *c.* 1830
Gilt and paste
Loaned indefinitely by Vere Laurie

Pot. Made by a Wedgwood potter on stage in *Chu-Chin-
Chow* (His Majesty's Theatre, London, 1916)
Earthenware
British Theatre Museum Association, given by
Reginald Cornish [1971/A/56]

Handkerchief. Used by Ellen Terry in *Othello*
(Lyceum Theatre, London, 1881)
Silk with embroidered strawberry motif
British Theatre Museum Association, given by
Barry Jones and Maurice Colbourne [1968/A/99]

Body of Les Paul guitar. Used in the making of *Tommy*,
and broken by Pete Townshend of The Who, *c.* 1969
Steel, wood, polymer resin
Given by Alan Smith [S.12–1978]

Crown. See Stage Jewellery above

Background:
Fan. Used by Mistinguett in a London revue, 1928
Ostrich feather [S.330–1979]

Stage properties may be specially designed to match the setting and costumes, and then made up by the property master. Alternatively, props from various productions may be salvaged from the property room (see centre top picture), or hired, bought, borrowed, or otherwise acquired. The degree of realism of the props reflects the nature of the production. In Henry Irving's Lyceum production of *The Bells* in 1878, for instance, a real stuffed pony, complete with mane and tail, was used as a prop in the 'vision scene'.

Another method of representing a horse a few years later is illustrated in the top left-hand corner, where a horse is being prepared for Mr. Herbert Campbell to ride in the pantomime *The Forty Thieves*, produced at Drury Lane on 26 December 1898. It was probably made with a *papiermâché* head and real horse-hair mane, the body being of brown paper over a chicken wire frame (the men in the picture are sticking the layers of paper together). The eyes would have been of coloured or painted glass, and the tail a piece of rope covered with cloth, with hair bound into it.

Larger-than-life pantomime productions demand exaggerated and striking props, such as the British lion (bottom left) and the double-headed creature with the large beaks (lower centre, inset). An example of a trick effect can be seen in the top right corner: Cassim Baba's untimely end had to be prepared in advance by making parts of his anatomy in sections, probably of *papiermâché* made in a cast, and possibly held together with gummed paper to enable it to be sliced by a sword. The genii and animal masks (centre left and right) were probably also made of *papiermâché*, then hand-painted and left to dry by the fire, as in the picture. Sawdust may well have been added to the paste to obtain a roughened texture, as described by Motley in the book *Theatre Props*. (*JA*)

Properties: Backstage 'Preparing for *The Forty Thieves* at Drury Lane, 1898'
Ralph Cleaver
Original artwork for *The Illustrated London News*,
24 December 1898
Pen, ink, Chinese white 380 × 270
Ingram Bequest

The rehearsal period is the time when ideas are exchanged between actors and director, when people and personalities gel – the period of creativity during which order emerges from initial chaos. Few outsiders are privileged to watch this process, since many actors feel exposed and vulnerable in rehearsal, and during the early stages often prefer not to be watched, even by other actors. The key person is the director: he has to be well acquainted with the text of the play and with the background material relating to the production, so that he can answer any queries and keep an overall view at all times. He must co-ordinate not only the various interpretations of the play by the actors but also the technical aspects of production such as design, lighting, and sound.

The first picture here shows Bernard Shaw directing Harley Granville-Barker and Lillah McCarthy at the dress rehearsal of *Androcles and the Lion*. Barker had directed throughout the earlier rehearsals, but now Shaw arrived and proceeded to turn Barker's careful instructions upside-down. Hesketh Pearson says of the occasion: 'In the course of four hours Shaw transformed the play from a comedy into an extravaganza. He danced about the stage, spouting bits from all parts with folded arms, turned our serious remarks into amusing quips and our funniments into tragedies, always exaggerating so as to prevent us from imitating him, and making us all feel we were acting in a charade'.

It was once the fashion for the director to arrive at the first rehearsal with all the moves prepared. Now, he is more likely to have an initial period of discussion and improvised exercises with actors. Some actors, however, still prefer to arrive at the first rehearsal with their lines already learnt – such as Laurence Olivier, noted for his meticulous preparations for a part, and shown here schooling Robert Lang, who took over his role of Shylock in October 1970 in Jonathan Miller's production of *The Merchant of Venice*.

Whereas the director of a play is usually working on a script by some one else, the choreographer of a ballet is composing an original work as he rehearses. Glen Tetley, who is shown here rehearsing Vergie Derman in *Field Figures* (1970), says: 'I find all my stimulus in bodies. . . . I start a ballet at the beginning, but never know precisely where it is going to land up. . . . When I come to work on a ballet . . . scores I have loved, incidents, things suddenly make connections that I never put a connection to before: sometimes there comes a wonderful state when everything starts to have meaning for me . . .'. Thus, as the dancer responds to the requirements of the choreographer a close relationship can develop, and in successful partnerships the stimulus of the dancer provides new inspiration for the choreographer, and in turn the dancer is pushed to new forms of physical expression. *(ER)*

Rehearsals
Laurice Olivier rehearsing Robert Lang for the role of
Shylock in Jonathan Miller's production of
The Merchant of Venice (Old Vic, London, 1970)
Photograph by Anthony Crickmay

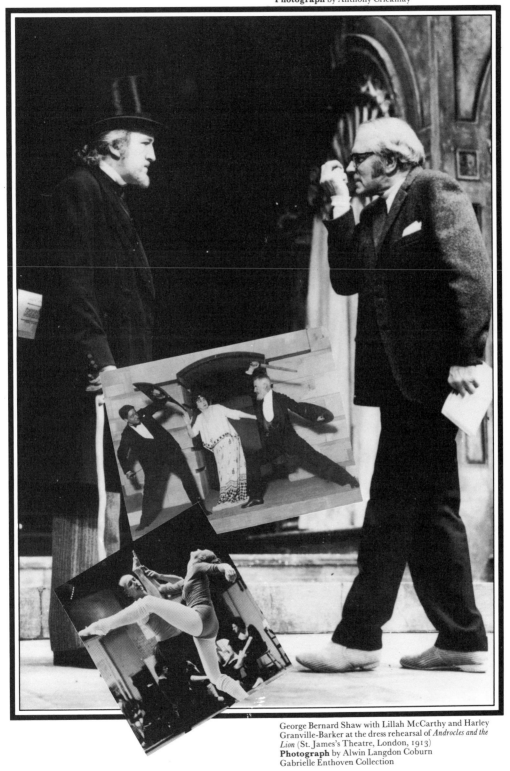

George Bernard Shaw with Lillah McCarthy and Harley
Granville-Barker at the dress rehearsal of *Androcles and the
Lion* (St. James's Theatre, London, 1913)
Photograph by Alwin Langdon Coburn
Gabrielle Enthoven Collection

Glen Tetley rehearsing Vergie Derman in *Field Figures*
(Theatre Royal, Nottingham, 1970)
Photograph by Anthony Crickmay

Acting and theatregoing were often dangerous and uncomfortable occupations before the invention of electric light. The first Drury Lane, an indoor theatre built in 1663, had a cupola to admit natural light but candles were its main source of illumination. Candles lit both auditorium and stage, since the idea of lighting the stage area alone did not evolve until the later nineteenth century.

The engraving opposite of Covent Garden (1763) shows five chandeliers hung over the stage; branched candelabra between the stage boxes, which would also have been situated around the front of the circle; and candles for the orchestra. The clarity with which the artist records the scene is deceptive, since the number of candles lighting the stage area probably only gave the equivalent light of one 100-watt bulb – ridiculously dim by modern standards.

Oil lamps were used in conjunction with candles towards the end of the eighteenth century, but by the 1820s many London theatres had installed gas jets. Gas 'floats' or footlights, hissing and flickering, replaced the twin-wick oil pots which had previously lit the forestage, and despite frequent accidents and explosions theatres persevered with gas.

New techniques and lighting effects were developed, however, perhaps the most important being that of limelight, perfected by Macready at Drury Lane in 1837. By burning a stick of quicklime in a gas jet it was possible to direct a single, brilliant beam onto the stage, varying its colour with sheets of glass. An equal mixture of oxygen and hydrogen was needed to produce the very hot flame needed to burn the lime, and each gas was kept in a separate bag, its mixture being controlled with pressure boards by the limelight man, who, as in the second engraving, usually worked from the fly-gallery.

Henry Irving, insisting that the quality of limelight was far superior to that of electric spotlights, took gas equipment on tour with him to theatres already using electricity, and at Drury Lane limelight was used for some effects as late as 1935. But Richard D'Oyly Carte, advertising his new theatre, the Savoy, which opened in 1881, emphasized among his innovative 'improvements' that for the first time all parts of his theatre were lit by electricity – and his programme even carried a light-bulb motif (see No. 88). Although he installed gas as a back-up system and had to overcome initial public scepticism and technical problems, Carte's faith in electricity was justified. A hundred years later theatrical lighting has reached extreme flexibility and sophistication, as in the temporary set-up at the Royal Festival Hall illustrated, where as many as a dozen banks of spotlights and floodlights include up to 400 bulbs of 1,000 watts each, all controlled by a computer console, operated by one man. *(CH)*

Electric Light at a rehearsal of the London Festival Ballet (Royal Festival Hall, London, 1980)
Photograph by Moira Walters

Candlelight in Covent Garden Theatre, depicted during a performance of Arne's opera *Artaxerxes*, 24 February 1763
After L. Boitard
Engraving published by E. Sumpter 189 × 260
Stone Collection

Limelight being operated in a nineteenth-century theatre
Detail from a reproduction in *The Illustrated Sporting and Dramatic News*, 1876
H. Sargent after F. Villiers
Engraving cut to 245 × 330
Gabrielle Enthoven Collection

This cartoon, published in 1779, features the dressing of an actress for the part of Macheath in John Gay's *The Beggar's Opera*, the ballad opera first performed in 1728. Though normally played by a man, it was also a popular 'breeches' part – a convention which arose when actresses were introduced to the English stage in the Restoration, as a means of showing off their legs. Several women had played Macheath in the 1730s, and Mrs. Farrell appeared in the role at Covent Garden on 17 October 1777.

Dressers today come under the control of the wardrobe department just as they did in the eighteenth century. Fourteen male dressers were recorded in 1757–60 at Covent Garden, but in 1766–67 there is reference only to eleven female dressers under the supervision of Mrs. Gould, head of the women's wardrobe. The husband of one of the dressers was men's wardrobe keeper. Nowadays dressers still tend to be linked to theatres rather than to individuals, and only some star performers employ their own dressers. At Covent Garden there is a rota system in operation, so that even the most junior dresser gets the chance to dress principals.

The dressers' work not only concerns being ready at the half-hour before the show and dressing performers after they have completed their make-up, but getting them anything else they need and looking after personal props. Though most dressing is done in the dressing-rooms, roles with many changes have to be dressed in the wings and sometimes even on stage – the latter particularly in pantomimes and musicals. In the theatre some dressing is cross-sexed, with men dressing women and vice versa, particularly on the Continent, but in opera and ballet this is rarely the case.

The character of Norman in Ronald Harwood's play *The Dresser* (1980) dwells on the emotional ties of the personal dresser with the actor, and Michael Redgrave draws attention to the theatricality of the relationship in his book *Mask or Face*: 'Like all good actors, good dressers have personalities which they can shed – if ever the phrase were valid it is here – at the drop of a hat. They know when to talk and when not to talk. They know when they are wanted and when to disappear. I would like to say they never forget anything. They seldom do. When they do, for them it is a bad performance. These attendant spirits, when they are good, are worth their weight in ticket stubs. When they are not good they may not be horrid but they have to go. Their relationship with the actor is like a long and perilous betrothal. Trust and fear are intermingled.' *(CEH)*

An ACTRESS at her Toilet. or MISS BRAZEN juſt BREECHT.
From the Original Picture by John Collet, in the poſſeſſion of Carington Bowles.
103
Printed for & Sold by CARINGTON BOWLES at his Map & Print Warehouſe N°69 in St Pauls Church Yard LONDON. Published as the Act dire. 24 June 17

The Dresser. 'An Actress at her Toilet, or Miss Brazen just Breecht '
Anonymous, after John Collet.
Published by Carington Bowles, 24 June 1779
Aquatint, coloured by hand. Cut to dimensions
355 × 257
Harry R. Beard Theatre Collection. f.64–12

This quick-life sketch shows the Polish ballet dancer Stanislas Idzikowski in the early stages of making-up in his dressing-room at the Coliseum for the short ballet *The Roses*, first performed there on 15 September 1924. The artist, Laura Knight (1877–1970), made other sketches of the principals and also designed the costumes. Ballet make-up lays emphasis on the cheekbones, lips, and above all the eyes – the line of the eyes and brows usually being extended with an upward lilt.

Make-up was originally used more for disguise than to enhance the natural features – for example, whitening for ghosts and blacking for negroes. According to Muriel St. Clare Byrne, make-up to enhance the natural appearance was introduced with the advent of the actress in 1660, and became a necessity when candles were superseded as a form of stage lighting in the nineteenth century, first by gas and then by electricity, which drains the face of natural colour.

Early make-up techniques used powder paints, either mixed with liquid or applied dry in one of two ways – directly on to the face or on a grease base. The whites and chromes contained lead which could be dangerous, sometimes fatal. *The Musical World* of 1864 blames a substance containing white lead, used to whiten the beard, for the death of the Belgian opera singer Zelger by slow blood-poisoning. A few years later, in 1873, Ludwig Leichner, a Wagnerian opera singer, set up in business manufacturing greasepaints in round sticks made from lead-free colours which he had evolved with assistance from the University of Warzburg some eight years previously: his grease-paints were also much simpler to apply as they could be blended easily with the finger-tips. By producing a wide range of prepared colours, he revolutionized stage make-up and his products are still used today.

Although greasepaint is still frequently used, during this century the 'pan-cake' products of firms such as Max Factor have come into their own. 'Pan-cake' is applied with a wet sponge which makes it quicker and easier to get a smooth surface. In films and television Max Factor reigns supreme, and the specialized make-up required for these media is applied by experts. In the theatre, artists usually do their own make-up.

Good make-up is a form of art, and for many actors and actresses the expressiveness of their make-up increases as the interpretation of their role develops. Character make-up may take some time to evolve, as John Gielgud observes in *Early Stages*: 'One's expression in a character part develops tremendously quickly after the first few times of making-up. Photographs taken at a dress rehearsal only show a kind of mask, a sketch of the actor's intention, just like his performance at an early rehearsal.' The make-up has to be worked on, along with everything else that goes into creating a good performance. *(CEH)*

Make-up: 'Idjikowski making up coliseum sept 1924'
Laura Knight
Charcoal 360 × 252. [S.309–1980]

This glimpse behind the scenes is of Lanner's ballet version of *Faust,* produced at the Empire Theatre in 1895. The label 'OP' (which means on the right-hand side facing the audience, opposite where the prompter usually sits) ensured the correct placing of the scenery by the stage hands, 60 of whom were employed at the Empire.

In the cramped conditions the general impression is one of activity and anticipation. Madame Zanfretta, the Mephistofoles, and Madame Cavallazzi, the Faust, are talking on the right. On the left is the character of Marguerite, with drummer soldiers in the foreground. As *The Sketch* article which featured this illustration says: 'Colours and costumes were blending in picturesque confusion, and, as the stage was in semi-darkness, the strong masked lights threw shadows against columns, or scattered them upon the ground'. The writer seems to have been captivated by backstage life, and even asked if he could understudy the stage manager.

Crowded scenes such as this are not as common backstage as they used to be. Nowadays there is little call for 'extras', nor is there need for an army of stage hands – and the lighting men have long since left the fly gallery for the comfort of an auditorium control room. 'Go behind' at a modern play, and likely as not the backstage area will be virtually deserted for much of the time.

Yet if you are fortunate enough, standing in the wings can still be exciting, especially during a busy scene. There is the pleasure of identifying actors disguised in make-up or strange wigs, or of watching a chorus filling the wings waiting for their cue and then entering the stage together. When it comes to the performance, rivalry and personality differences must be put aside, and the professional spirit takes over. *(CEH)*

Backstage. 'The OP Side of the Empire', 1895
Louis Gunnis
Original artwork for *The Sketch*, 1 January 1896
Pencil, watercolour, and chinese white 366 × 273
Ingram Bequest

PROGRAMMES, POSTERS AND PUBLICITY

All the effort and expense involved in mounting a production are likely to come to nothing unless it is properly marketed. Publicity has always had a vital role to play in the theatre, particularly at times when money is tight and grants uncertain. West End shows in 1980 were costing anything from £50,000 for a low-budget play to over £500,000 for a big musical, and continuing inflation makes effective publicity crucial.

Theatre publicity is not a recent innovation. In medieval times productions of mystery plays were 'advertised' in advance by proclamation, and then by a procession of management, costumed actors, and musicians, who paraded the streets bearing banners to attract as much attention as possible. In essence, this two-pronged approach is not dissimilar from that adopted by a modern subsidized theatre like the Royal Court. About one month before a first night, press releases are issued. The intervening weeks are then occupied with preparations for the build-up to the opening: getting posters and leaflets ready for distribution; booking advertising space in newspapers and possibly on buses; issuing special publicity to minority groups to whom the show is likely to be of interest; and persuading the press to devote space to feature articles. Whereas subsidized theatres usually have their own publicity department, commercial managements will generally hire an agency to mount a publicity campaign tailored for each show.

When the Royal Shakespeare Company's *Nicholas Nickleby* opened on Broadway in 1981, it received advance saturation coverage in the media – but played to only 38.5 per cent capacity during previews. Although the papers (with the exception of the influential *New York Times*) gave it rave first-night reviews, by the end of the following week attendance had risen to only 68.7 per cent. When *The New York Times* published a second, more favourable review, attendance jumped to 85 per cent capacity – and after a third review to 100 per cent. To what extent *The New York Times* depressed a popular response it was then forced to endorse is a matter of controversy.

If a show is generally panned by the critics a frantic campaign of extra advertising and ticket discounts may be mounted in order to create audiences through good word-of-mouth. Although this is an expensive and risky gamble it sometimes pays off: *Charlie Girl* and *No Sex Please, We're British* are legendary examples of West End shows that survived initial critical hostility to become long-running hits.

Finding a new audience for every new show by 'blanket' advertising has become such a costly business that more efficient alternatives are being sought and tried out. Among the most attractive are subscription schemes, in which season tickets are offered at discounts of up to one-third. These create a nucleus of support not just for one production but for a whole season, and often lead to regular attendance in the long term. They bring in a healthy cash advance to theatres, lessening their dependence on last-minute ticket sales. Birmingham Repertory Theatre, for example, which adopted subscription booking in 1978, had 33,000 more people attending in 1979–80 than in the previous year, representing an increase in box-office takings of almost 50 per cent. With the advance money subscription schemes bring in, theatres can plan with more confidence. What is not certain is whether in their desire to please regular patrons they will tend to choose 'safer' plays than might otherwise have been attempted.

The RSC and the National Theatre find that their most cost-effective form of publicity is to send out brochure-booking forms to members who pay to be on their mailing lists. With the aid of a computer the RSC offers in this way preferential booking to around 35,000 people, who in 1980 bought 30 per cent of the seats in advance at the Aldwych and 40 per cent of those at Stratford. This can be combined with a specific drive aimed at minority audiences: in 1978 the National Theatre offered *Time Out* readers a special discount on tickets for its premiere of Bond's *The Woman*. 'Student Standby' schemes were first introduced in the mid-1970s. These account for six to seven per cent of all tickets sold by the RSC – about 20,000 students attendances per year. In 1979 West End commercial theatres adopted a similar scheme which resulted in 140,000 students attending in the first twelve months.

The introduction of fresh marketing and publicity techniques by big subsidized theatres has lessened their dependence on traditional forms of advertising. Posters, for instance, play a minor role at the National Theatre, being produced principally to decorate front-of-house and adjoining sites, and for sale as souvenirs. But for fringe theatre groups posters remain a vital form of publicity: cheap to produce and to over-print, they can account for up to 50 per cent of their audiences. Circuses likewise rely heavily on posters and often exploit familiar images, playing on traditional expectations of the sawdust ring (No. 89). Their appeal is still made through pictures rather than words, as in the poster advertising a menagerie in the eighteenth century (No. 80). Eye-catching in a very different way are the flyposters for pop concerts (No. 85), whose brilliant 'day-glo' colours light up derelict sites.

Methods of selling tickets are being radically rethought: purchase by credit card over the telephone is now standard practice, as is the sale in London of half-price tickets from the booth opened in 1980 in Leicester Square by the Society of West End Theatre. In the same year the Palace Theatre, Manchester, installed the new Box Office Computer System which is capable of printing tickets as they are sold, and of recommending the best available seats. This dispenses with the master booking sheet marked by one person, and makes it easier to sell tickets simultaneously from several terminals. The computer also allows instant audits of ticket sales, and is able to maintain a mailing list. Future plans include linking the BOCS system to British Telecom's computer, Prestel, and making it possible to book theatre seats by telephone from information flashed on one's television screen. *(JF)*

Printed playbills, to be posted up in towns, inns, and coffee houses, were in existence from Shakespeare's day, although few prior to 1700 are extant. The earliest bills would have been handwritten, and more publicity was announced by word of mouth. By 1700 bills were usually printed, although they did not generally give the year of performance until the 1760s. Despite the handwritten note on the playbill opposite that it dates from 1725, research has proved the correct date to be 1718, which makes it one of the oldest playbills in the Theatre Museum.

In addition to these small bills giving advance publicity, considerably fewer 'great bills' were printed and displayed outside the theatres nearer the performance date. The note on this bill, 'With Entertainments of Singing and Dancing, as will be Express'd in the Great Bill', alerted the public to look for more details on the larger bill that was coming shortly at Drury Lane.

This bill advertises a benefit performance for Mrs. Saunders (1686–c.1745), an actress whose illness forced her early retirement in 1721. She was renowned for her lively portrayal of chambermaids – hence the choice of a popular comedy by Beaumont and Fletcher, which doubtless enabled her to display her talents to the full. As beneficiary she was entitled to the proceeds of the performance, less the house charges of £40 or more. She stood to gain perhaps twice that amount if a lot of tickets had been sold in advance – and she herself would have sold as many as possible.

The play began 'exactly at Six a-Clock', the starting time for much of the eighteenth century, midway between the afternoon presentation of plays customary in the previous century and the modern convention of evening performance.

The warning partly visible at the bottom of the bill was directed at patrons who refused to confine themselves to the auditorium: '[By His Majesties] Command, No Persons are to be admitted behind the [Scenes] . . .', and informed them: '[nor any] Money to be Return'd after [the Curtain is drawn up]'. This refers to the generous practice current in some theatres of the time whereby the audience could listen to the prologue, music, or even see a whole act before deciding whether they wanted to leave and have their money returned. *(CH)*

(1725)

For the Benefit of Mrs SAUNDERS.

By His Majesty's Company of Comedians. *1725.*

AT THE

THEATRE ROYAL

In *Drury-Lane* :

On MONDAY the 14th Day of *April,*
will be prefented, *(In the Time of Wilks, and Mrs Oldfield)*

A COMEDY call'd,

Rule a Wife, and Have a Wife.

With Entertainments of Singing and Dancing,
as will be Exprefs'd in the Great Bill.

To begin exactly at Six a-Clock.

~~His Ma~~ *~~jef~~* ~~ties Command, No Perfons are to be admitted behind the~~
~~~~ *money to be Return'd after*

Early Playbill
Theatre Royal in Drury Lane, 14 April 1718
Letterpress 209 × 178
Gabrielle Enthoven Collection

Illustrated bills, the forerunners of modern posters, were not common in England before the nineteenth century. They were introduced to publicize entertainments with the widest popular appeal such as circus, menageries, and magic. With bold images they caught the attention of those who could not have read an entirely lettered bill.

The woodcuts of the animals in Pidcock's Travelling Menagerie are by Thomas Bewick (1753–1828), an artist who excelled in portraying animals. Bewick had a rare opportunity to draw exotic beasts from life in 1788, when his home town of Newcastle was visited by a large menagerie – possibly that of Gilbert Pidcock, who had exhibited animals at fairs in London and the provinces since c.1769. Pidcock became so successful that he bought out Clark's menagerie based at Exeter Exchange, London, in 1793, and presented 'the greatest Assemblage of Foreign Birds and Beasts ever exhibited in the Kingdom', in addition to his touring shows. This poster dates from c. 1795, although it could have been displayed for a season or more, offsetting the initial expense of using Bewick's illustrations.

At Pidcock's Menagerie for one shilling (servants sixpence), the public could see fabulous animals such as the 'Real Unicorn' or Rhinocerous, and the Elephant that cost 1,000 guineas. Pidcock, 'the Modern Noah' with his 'Wonderful Ark' at Exeter Exchange (built in the late seventeenth century as a shopping arcade), attracted the crowds to his shows until his death in 1810. A menagerie continued at Exeter Exchange under new management, but by 1831 the heyday of the menagerie was over. The animals, by now familiar to the public, were sold to the Surrey Zoological Gardens.

The second bill features a woodcut by an anonymous artist which shows the Scottish magician, John Henry Anderson (1814–1874), performing his 'Unlucky Umbrella' trick. Known as 'The Great Wizard of the North', Anderson's brilliance as a performer was matched by his flair for publicity. Each magical feat is described in antiquated or pseudo-scientific language that conjures up a sense of mystery, and the illustrations on the bills were changed regularly to publicize his many tricks.

Conjuring was popular at fairs during the eighteenth century and became a lucrative theatrical concern in the nineteenth. Anderson amazed Londoners in 1840 with his bullet-catching trick, and was one of the first magicians to conjure a rabbit from a hat.

(CH)

Illustrated bills advertising menagerie and magic
Thomas Bewick, c. 1795
Woodcut and letterpress 644 × 250
Gabrielle Enthoven Collection

Anonymous
Theatre Royal, Adelphi, London, 14 June 1841
Woodcut and letterpress 503 × 246
Gabrielle Enthoven Collection

These bills, from Liverpool and Glasgow, are examples of the conventional form of theatrical advertisement in the mid-nineteenth century. Unlike the menagerie and magic bills on the previous page, their visual impact does not depend on appealing illustrations but on artful use of typography. The names of the Keans dominate the bill for the Saturday performance of *Romeo and Juliet*, even though their appearance was not until the following Monday – in *Richard III*. As a further inducement to potential patrons the bill offers gallery places at half-price in an attempt to combat fierce competition from local theatres.

The Glasgow bill concentrates less on the performers, despite the fact that Mario, Santley, and Titiens were outstanding singers of their day, emphasizing instead that this is the last chance to see the 'Italian Opera'. This form of entertainment was so popular that it was customary to use the term 'Italian Opera' to attract the public even when the opera was not strictly Italian: thus, Gounod's *Faust* was actually French, although it was sung in Italian on this occasion.

Stars from London regularly performed in the provinces in the later eighteenth century, and were popular attractions. The Liverpool Theatre opened in 1772 with a policy of only employing London actors, but by 1844 a stock company existed, acting with visiting 'stars' who were usually engaged for about a fortnight. Liverpool was independent of an established provincial circuit, unlike the Glasgow Theatre in Dunlop Street which opened in 1782 as part of a circuit that included Edinburgh, Aberdeen, and Dundee. By 1865 Glasgow too had its stock actors and musicians – capable of performing plays, but only of filling minor roles in foreign opera. Since a fashion for this had begun in the 1820s, London managements supplied the demand by sending whole casts on tour, especially when rail travel became available.

Both bills opposite are headed with engravings of the Royal Arms, since each theatre had been granted Patents allowing dramatic performances – Liverpool in 1768 and Glasgow in 1829. Until the Theatres Act of 1843, only theatres in possession of such patents could properly call themselves 'Royal' or produce 'legitimate' drama. Once this monopoly had ended, managements had to contend with new rivalry and it became all the more important for them to produce eye-catching bills such as these. *(CH)*

Mid nineteenth-century playbills
Theatre Royal, Liverpool, 9 November 1844
Letterpress 547 × 226
Gabrielle Enthoven Collection

Theatre Royal, Glasgow, 13 October 1865
Letterpress 506 × 250
Gabrielle Enthoven Collection

John Hassall designed the poster opposite for *The Only Way*, a dramatization of Dickens's novel *A Tale of Two Cities*, for the original production at the Lyceum Theatre on 16 February 1899. John Martin-Harvey starred as the hero Sydney Carton, who is here portrayed moments before his execution. In contrast to the earlier menagerie (*c.* 1795) and magic bills (1841), in which words and illustrations are equally important, the image is now completely dominant. By the late nineteenth century detailed information which had hitherto appeared on bills was usually contained in theatre programmes, and did not have to be duplicated in posters.

This poster was produced with a blank space for overprinting the relevant theatre and dates, and would have been used on tour. It demonstrates the new clarity and linear quality introduced in posters of the 1890s: the hero's figure is emphasized by his stark white coat, which contrasts with the surrounding tones of brown, grey, and green. Stylized flat areas of yellow and grey delineate the sky, while the cut-off foreground figures and the use of the guillotine and steps to frame and emphasize the figure recall the Japanese prints that Hassall admired. The blood-red kerchiefs of the crowd add symbolically chilling touches of colour.

Theatrical posters without a mass of printed information became popular in the late nineteenth century, the most important forerunner being Frederick Walker's poster for *The Woman in White* (1871), which was a large black and white woodcut, still featuring shading and three-dimensional effects. In the 1890s under the influence of Jules Chéret and Toulouse-Lautrec, poster designs became bolder and two-dimensional, in a manner used effectively for the first time by an English artist in Aubrey Beardsley's 1894 Avenue Theatre poster (see No. 88).

John Hassall (1868–1948), later known as 'the poster king', trained as an artist in Antwerp and Paris, only discovering his flair for poster art when a firm of colour printers requested sample designs from artists. The development of colour lithography and new high-speed printing processes, combined with a boom in advertising, had created a demand for poster art.

Hassall, along with the Bickerstaffs and Dudley Hardy, was one of the most successful British artists to adopt the new style of poster design used by Beardsley, and by the turn of the century poster design had become an established art form. Frederick Walker's remarks were prophetic when he referred to his 1871 poster as 'a first attempt at what I consider might develop into a most important branch of art'. *(CH)*

Late nineteenth-century poster
John Hassall
Lithograph 794 × 465
Gabrielle Enthoven Collection

This huge poster is one of a pair designed by Jean Cocteau in 1911 and used for the sixth Paris season of Diaghilev's Ballets Russes during May and June 1913. Sparingly designed, with a sense of wit and movement, it depicts the ravishing ballerina Karsavina as the young girl in Fokine's ballet *Le Spectre de la rose*. Large and eye-catching, with a white figure on a blue background and red lettering, Cocteau's poster captures the spirit of Karsavina's dancing, as Chéret's had of Moulin Rouge dancers and Toulouse-Lautrec's of Loïe Fuller.

Le Spectre de la rose, first performed at the Théâtre de Monte Carlo on 19 April 1911, was brought to the Théâtre du Châtelet later that year. For this Paris season, the impresario Gabriel Astruc, Diaghilev's sponsor in Paris, wanted new publicity material, and asked Bakst to design a poster. Bakst declined, recommending instead the twenty-year-old Cocteau. Although Diaghilev was in favour of re-using the poster depicting Pavlova designed by Serov in 1909, which had advertised his previous Paris seasons, Astruc persisted and commissioned preliminary sketches from Cocteau.

Pavlova had left the company by this time, and Cocteau's designs were for two posters representing Karsavina and Nijinsky in their respective roles in the new ballet *Le Spectre de la rose*. His small chinese-ink sketches were translated into large lithographs, signed on the stone by Cocteau, and the posters first appeared on the hoardings heralding the 1911 season at the Théâtre de Monte Carlo, and subsequently in Paris for the Théâtre du Châtelet season.

The posters were reproduced in the 1911 programme, and used again with appropriately altered lettering for the 1913 season at the Théâtre des Champs Elysées, Astruc's brand new theatre in the Avenue Montaigne. Unlike *The Only Way* poster on the previous page, these posters advertised the entire season of ballets instead of one production.

Cocteau (1889–1963), author, poet, and artist, was immediately attracted to the productions of the Ballets Russes when he saw their first Paris performance in May 1909, and he wanted to be associated with the company, particularly after his meeting with Diaghilev in 1909. 'From that moment I became a member of the company', he wrote enthusiastically, but although he was soon to collaborate by writing the libretto for *Le Dieu bleu*, it was not until 1911 that he wrote programme notes and designed their posters. *(CH)*

Early twentieth-century poster
Théâtre des Champs Elysées, Paris, 1913
Jean Cocteau
Lithograph 1995 × 1225
Given by Mademoiselle Lucienne Astruc and Richard
Buckle in memory of the collaboration between Diaghilev
and Gabriel Astruc. © SPADEM, Paris 1982

These posters advertising four post-war plays illustrate some developments in poster design over the last 30 years. In early poster production, hand-crafted processes such as lithography and screen-printing were favoured, and artists such as Cocteau and Hassall were called upon to produce designs for posters. With the increased use of mechanical processes for poster production in the 1940s and 1950s, theatrical publicity could be composed at the printer's without recourse to an independent designer, but by the 1960s creative artwork began again to feature more generally in poster design.

The posters for the original production of *The Mousetrap* (Ambassadors, 25 November 1953) and *The Entertainer* (Royal Court, 10 April 1957) concentrate on full printed details about the play titles, their authors and casts, but reveal nothing about the plays themselves. Reproduced photographs were popular in theatrical posters of the 1950s, and stage celebrities like Richard Attenborough and Sheila Sim, who could be seen on television, were also shown happily smiling down from the hoardings.

The lay-out of *The Entertainer* poster reveals more clearly the involvement of a graphic designer, and with its straight lines and blocks of orange, yellow, and black, it is reminiscent of a Mondrian painting. The same design was used by the Royal Court to illustrate all its 1957 and 1958 posters and programmes, whereas the programme cover for *The Mousetrap*, reproducing a drawing of a mousetrap, bore no relation to the poster design.

The designs of the silk-screen printed posters for *Equus* (Birmingham Rep, 26 March 1975) and *Cabaret* (Sheffield Crucible, 26 October 1977) were repeated on their programme covers. Unlike the two previous poster designs, each aimed to convey the style and atmosphere of the production. The designer of the *Equus* poster, Chris Frampton, used a photograph of a Bernini Vatican horse sculpture for her artwork: by stabbing the image with a knife and tearing from the central point of the eye, she laid the pieces slightly apart and added the lettering, thus creating a powerful poster to advertise a play about a boy who blinded horses. The image aims to startle – as does the poster for *Cabaret*, design by Eian McKay, then a student at Sheffield's Granville College of Art. He also based his poster on an existing image, using a Nazi-booted performer originally designed by Guy Peellaert (b. 1934) for a Crazy Horse cabaret poster in Paris, 1968. The figure is placed over the neon-like red and white lettering – which proclaims the name of the play seven times, but gives no author or cast details, despite the fact that this production starred Gemma Jones.

Not all modern theatre posters are as well-designed as these for *Equus* in Birmingham and *Cabaret* in Sheffield, and with escalating costs of colour-printing and hoarding space, and the variety of other publicity methods now available, their quality is in danger of decline. *(CH)*

Modern Posters
The Mousetrap
Ambassadors Theatre, London, 1953
Offset 505 × 318

The Entertainer
Royal Court Theatre, London, 1957
Offset and letterpress 505 × 318

AMBASSADORS THEATRE, West St. Cambridge Circus, w.c.2
Sole Proprietors: Ambassadors Theatre Ltd.   Lessees: J. W. Pemberton & Co. Ltd.
Managing Directors: W. G. Curtis & H. J. Malden.
Licenced by the Lord Chamberlain to J. F. H. Jay.

Monday to Friday: 7.30   Saturday: 5.15 and 8.0   Tuesday: 2.30   BOX OFFICE
Stalls: 15/-, 10/6, 8/6;   Dress Circle: 15/-, 10/6, 8/6, 5/6;   Pit (unreserved): 3/6.   Temple Bar 1171

Peter Saunders presents

Richard Attenborough
Sheila Sim in

THE MOUSETRAP
by Agatha Christie

Royal Court
Theatre

English Stage Company
Artistic Director George Devine

April 10th
to
May 11th

Laurence Olivier
Dorothy Tutin
George Relph
Brenda de Banzie
in
The Entertainer
by
John Osborne

Audrey Dexter   Vivienne Drummond
Stanley Meadows   Richard Pasco

Director: Tony Richardson

Setting: Alan Tagg

All seats bookable

Spencer

Dexter

O'Doherty

26 March–5 April
14–25 April
at the
Birmingham Rep

EQUUS
Peter Shaffer

cor by Roger Furse

CABARET
CABARET
CABARET
RET
ARET
ABARET
ABARET
ABARET

Equus
Birmingham Repertory Theatre, 1975
Chris Frampton
Silk screen 761 × 508

Cabaret
Crucible Theatre, Sheffield, 1977
Eian McKay (after Guy Peellaert)
Silk screen 760 × 509

Constantly changing, posters advertising rock concerts and record releases appear on illegal sites in every town. Corrugated fencing, building-site screens, and blank walls offer tempting free space to the entertainment promoter. With fluorescent colours, uncompromising images, and bold typography, they proclaim singers and groups from Lene Lovich to The Osmonds: the larger the image or lettering, the more effective the poster. Often ignored by hurrying commuters, freshly-posted bills decorate ugly hoardings, but when rainsoaked and torn their effect is depressing.

Little annoyance was caused by bills attached to any wall or post until the nineteenth century, when the rapid expansion of advertising resulted in an overwhelming profusion of huge posters. Newly posted, they were immediately covered with those of rivals, and fights between billstickers sometimes ensued. To guarantee advertising space, contractors began to erect hoardings, a popular practice from the 1870s onwards, and one which became very profitable. The annual charge for hoarding space in 1899 could be as much as £300. Today's hoarding space costs as much for a month, but the only cost involved in illegal posting is the flyposter's fee of about 50 pence for every poster displayed.

Although the Advertising Regulations Bill of 1907 made flyposting illegal, police in central London rarely have time to prosecute. 'We have better things to do': and flyposters rarely linger to test the truth of the officer's claim. To avoid being challenged for suspicious behaviour, they prefer to work in daylight rather than by night, and their methods often resemble those of the artful billsticker described in 1875: 'sticking his notices and disappearing with marvellous rapidity. And how he would chuckle as he drove away, more especially if he had succeeded in covering over the handiwork of a rival.' *(CH)*

Illegal poster site: 43 Harrington Road, London SW7,
seen at monthly intervals from January to March 1980
Photographs by Moira Walters

The earliest theatre tickets were made of metal, and although possibly used in ancient Greece, they were not introduced in Britain until the seventeenth century. In 1660 Davenant introduced a system of admission whereby a metal ticket check, purchased at the door, was presented at the entrance to the pit, box, or gallery. This scheme only partly succeeded, since obstinate occupants of the boxes resisted payment before the end of the first act until c. 1740.

The square copper ticket illustrated, c. 1840, gives only essential information:'TR PIT EOH' – issued for the pit at the Theatre Royal English Opera House. The circular brass ticket (Bath, Theatre Royal, c. 1800) is stamped 'SECOND PRICES', and was available for those seeing the second half of the programme only. Wealthy patrons could buy a beautifully engraved silver General Ticket for £100 or more which permitted entry for years: the oval one illustrated was issued at Drury Lane in 1795 – for expiry in 1896!

Ivory and bone tickets, late eighteenth-century innovations, were also used as season tickets. The circular bone pass shown was issued c. 1800 for Grimaldi's box at Sadler's Wells (to which privilege Grimaldi was entitled as a performer earning more than £6 a week). The three ivory tickets are pierced for ribbons and engraved with the purchaser's name, the gold mounted one once belonging to Lord Nelson's nephew.

Card tickets date back to at least 1716, and were first issued for benefits and special occasions. Shown to prospective buyers, their attractive designs and colours made them persuasive advertisements – for example, the tickets for Mr. Mathews's Night (Drury Lane, 1808), authenticated by the actor, and The Grand Masque (King's Theatre, 1811), printed respectively in maroon and red. Some tickets even offered free wine or punch to the bearer (Sadler's Wells c. 1800).

When theatre seats came to be numbered in the later nineteenth century, the modern stub variety superseded other kinds. Form and design of theatre tickets have changed little since the Gaiety ticket was printed on card c. 1890, although paper tickets are now the rule, some currently being issued by computers – while a few theatres, such as Covent Garden and Drury Lane, still prefer the more luxurious medium of card. In contrast, pop concert organizers have tried dispensing with formal tickets altogether, stamping spectators' hands with a rubber stamp mark as they pay their entrance money. *(CH)*

Theatre tickets and passes from the late eighteenth century to the present day
Gabrielle Enthoven Collection

S atin and silk programmes have been used for special theatrical performances since the late eighteenth century. The tradition continues today, particularly for royal occasions at the theatre – though sometimes nylon is used as a substitute for the more expensive silk and satin. Satin is particularly luxurious because it is heavy in texture with an attractive sheen on one side. On the glittering occasion celebrated opposite, the white satin programme complemented the décor of the passages and waiting rooms leading to the royal box; these were 'fitted up with white silk and festooned with natural flowers of the choicest kind', according to *The Illustrated London News*.

The first reigning English monarch to attend command performances in public theatres was Charles II, and Queen Victoria was an avid theatregoer who loved opera, melodrama, and above all, circus. After the death of Prince Albert in 1861 she ceased to attend public performances, but even then she commanded that certain performances should take place at the royal palaces.

This event, which took place at Her Majesty's Theatre on 20 July 1843, was truly a 'command' performance, since the Queen had expressly desired to see Fanny Elssler and Fanny Cerrito dance together. Elssler was one of the greatest stars of the Romantic ballet, and Cerrito was the current favourite with the London audiences. The result was a sensation; as a contemporary critic wrote: 'such a *pas de deux* was never witnessed before in the memory of the oldest opera frequenter'. Cerrito then appeared in her much acclaimed role as the water nymph in Perrot's ballet *Ondine*.

Another attraction of the evening was *Il Barbiere di Siviglia* performed by such outstanding opera singers as Giulia Grisi (whom the Queen idolized), Mario, and Lablache (No. 3). *(CH)*

BY COMMAND OF HER MOST GRACIOUS MAJESTY

THE QUEEN.

ON THURSDAY, JULY 20, 1843.

PROGRAMME OF THE PERFORMANCES.
ROSSINI'S OPERA OF

IL BARBIERE DI SIVIGLIA.

Rosina,	Made GRISI,
Il Conte d Almaviva,	Signor MARIO,
Bartolo,	Signor LABLACHE,
Basilio,	Signor F. LABLACHE,
Figaro,	Signor FORNASARI.

BETWEEN THE ACTS OF THE OPERA.

MADLLE FANNY ELSSLER   AND   MADLLE CERITO

WILL DANCE

A PAS DE DEUX,

(Composed expressly for this occasion, by M. PERROT.)

To conclude with the Grand Ballet, (in Six Tableaux) by M. PERROT, the Music by Signor PUGNI, entitled

ONDINE;

OU,

LA NAIADE,

THE SCENERY BY MR. WILLIAM GRIEVE

PRINCIPAL DANCERS AND CHARACTERS.

MADLLE CERITO,

Mesdlles CAMILLE,   SCHEFFER,   PLANQUET,   BENARD,   GALBY,   DUCIE,   COPERE,

AND

MADLLE GUY STEPHAN,

M. ST. LEON,   AND   M. PERROT.

1st TABLEAU—(La Coquille) Ballabile, by the CORPS DE BALLET.
    Pas de Quatre, Mesdlles GUY STEPHAN, GALBY, BENARD, and DUCIE.
    Pas Scenique d'Entrainement, by Madlle CERITO.
3rd TABLEAU—(La Vision) Pas des Ondes, by the whole CORPS DE BALLET.
    Pas de Six, Mesdlles CERITO, CAMILLE, SCHEFFER, GALBY, BENARD, and M. ST. LEON.
    (Composed by Mlle CERITO)
4th TABLEAU—(Fete de la Madonne,) Grand Tarentelle, by the whole CORPS DE BALLET.
    Pas de Quatre, Mesdlles GUY STEPHAN, CAMILLE, PLANQUET, and M. PERROT.
    Pas de L'Ombre, by Madlle CERITO.
6th TABLEAU—(La Rose Fletrie) Saltarelle, by Madlle CERITO and M. PERROT.

**Programme for Queen Victoria's first State Visit
to the theatre**
Her Majesty's Theatre, London, 20 July 1843
White satin with gilt metallic fringe
360 × 258 (including fringe)
Gabrielle Enthoven Collection

Theatre programmes have varied enormously in form and design since the mid-nineteenth century, when the pamphlet programme as we know it was first introduced. A printed broadsheet giving the plot, or the prologue or epilogue of a play, was sometimes available in the seventeenth century, but it was not until the early eighteenth that details of casts began to appear on playbills which the public could buy. These, sold outside and inside theatres by orange-sellers, served both as poster and programme until they became too large for easy reference.

Silk and satin programmes had been introduced for galas and benefits since the late eighteenth century, but paper programmes did not appear until about 1850. At first they were simply smaller versions of the playbill printed daily, such as the Haymarket programme (1851) at bottom right of the display opposite. It was perhaps their pungent smell of ink that inspired the perfumiers Rimmel, in about 1859, to produce more elegant scented programmes with borders punched to appear like lace, such as the Princess's programme (1866) at bottom centre. Both types of programme existed concurrently, the perfumed ones for wealthier patrons.

Other firms soon followed Rimmel's example of using programmes for advertising, so that by 1888 *The Playgoer* complained: 'To charge twopence or threepence for a poorly designed programme full of advertisements is simply wicked', and praised the few theatres who issued them free. Due to the paper shortage of the Second World War, programmes were then much reduced in size, like the Windmill programme of 1941 towards top left, but now they are booklets of a dozen or more advertisement-packed pages (although free single-sheet cast lists are offered as alternatives in some subsidized and fringe theatres).

Imaginative programme design is not unusual today, as for the Elton John concert tour programme (1976) at top left, but in the 1880s programmes with coloured designs were an innovation. Richard D'Oyly Carte led the way at his new Savoy Theatre, and his beautifully coloured programmes, issued free, incorporated a light-bulb motif in their design which reflected another of his innovations – a theatre lit entirely by electricity (see No. 75). Other managers issued novel programmes such as the golden egg-shaped one (Drury Lane, 1902), and some commissioned established artists to design posters and programmes; Aubrey Beardsley's poster design appeared on the 1894 Avenue Theatre programme at centre, and Bertram Mills commissioned Dudley Hardy's artwork for posters and programmes in 1920 (see No. 89). The *Twelfth Night* programme at left centre (Savoy, 1912) is illustrated with a reproduction of William Nicholson's costume design for Viola, while the cover for the 1938 Cochran revue at top right aims to reflect the glamour and polish of the entertainment. *(CH)*

British theatre programmes
Gabrielle Enthoven Collection

Dudley Hardy's striking image of a white-faced clown illustrates the programme cover and poster for the first circus Bertram Mills ever organized at Olympia, on 17 December 1920. After drawing this pencil and watercolour cartoon, Hardy (1866–1922) executed an intermediary oil painting which was then reproduced on the publicity material. Wearing traditional conical cap, ruff, pantaloons, and slippers, Hardy's clown wields the ringmaster's whip – an amusing reflection of the traditional friendly antagonism between clown and ringmaster.

The goose design on the clown's costume introduces another traditional note, since geese were often used in nineteenth-century pantomime. The clown's role as assistant to the equestrian acrobats is also suggested; standing on a stool, he holds the paper hoop or 'balloon' through which the acrobats will jump. An image of the Holborn Amphitheatre (see No. 97) shows this feat in action in the previous century.

Bertram Mills, a keen equestrian but not then a showman, visited a circus at Olympia in the 1919–20 Christmas season, decided that he could produce a better show, and promptly signed an agreement to do so the following year. An undertaker and coach-builder by trade, Mills put together a superb sixteen-act show including twelve clowns, Japanese gymnasts, Sanger's Elephants, Henning Orlando's Horses, trick cyclists, and a funfair. The show lived up to the promise of its publicity and Mills revealed his professional astuteness in choosing as his artist Dudley Hardy, who was by this time a popular illustrator of theatrical posters.

The quality and speed of Mills's show revitalized English circus and made it a newly prestigious form of entertainment. His repeated successes at Olympia led to the formation of a touring or 'tenting' circus in 1930, run by his sons Cyril and Bernard. They carried on the family business after their father's death in 1938, and apart from an enforced wartime break 'Bertram Mills' Circus' was presented every Christmas until unfavourable economic conditions forced it to close in 1966–67. *(CH)*

Preliminary design for publicity illustration for Bertram Mills' Circus, with original programme
Dudley Hardy
Pencil, watercolour, and bodycolour 439 × 316
Antony Hippisley Coxe Circus Collection

Programme: Olympia, London, 17 December 1920
244 × 185
Gabrielle Enthoven Collection

By the beginning of the twentieth century, the pamphlet type of theatre programme became the most popular format. Productions are generally characterized by the design on the programme cover rather than by its shape, with
the result that odd-shaped programmes (such as that for the Berliner Ensemble
at top left, in the form of a fan) are an exception. Some theatres prefer a standard cover
featuring a symbol (Comédie Française, Paris, 1970, at right centre), or an image of the
theatre itself (Bolshoi Theatre, Moscow, 1976, at bottom centre).

Other covers emphasize the star performers (Barbra Streisand in *Funny Girl*, Winter
Garden, New York, 1964, at bottom right), or try to evoke the atmosphere of a perfor-
mance by depicting costume or set designs. Bakst's design for Potiphar's costume in *La
Légende de Joseph* (top centre) was chosen to illustrate the programme for the Ballets
Russes in Madrid 1921, while that for *A Streetcar Named Desire* (Ethel Barrymore
Theatre, New York, 1957, at centre), bears a line drawing, brown on cream, evoking
the homeless Blanche outside a New Orleans house. This echoed the set design, and the
same cover with different colouring was used two years later when the play was first
produced in London.

Another convention is to repeat the poster design on the programme cover (Casino de
Paris, 1936, at top right), the image by Charles Kiffer of Maurice Chevalier wittily
depicting the popular star.

Advertisements, which first appeared in theatre programmes *c.* 1860, quickly became one of their standard features, along with chatty articles, biographical details, and
photographs of the cast, which had hitherto appeared only in the special souvenir programmes of the late nineteenth century. The earliest programme illustrated (Knicker-
bocker Theatre, New York, 1914) is full of advertisements, ranging from one for a rust-
proof corset to a delicately-coloured pastoral image advertising Parisian perfume which,
the manufacturer regrets, is difficult to obtain during wartime.

A balance between advertisement and information is achieved in the 1930s programmes, which include photographs and articles and are attractive souvenirs of the
performance. The 26-page Monte Carlo programme (1937) at left of centre was used
for the whole season of ballet, inserts being added for each particular performance,
while its cover, designed by Jean Gabriel Doumergue, was originally a travel poster,
intended to capture the *chic* stylishness of the resort. This kind of programme – a basic
'core' with special covers and inserts relating to the particular production, as also used
here for *A Streetcar Named Desire* and *Funny Girl* – was developed as a monthly publication
by *Playbill*, and is now used by many managements in New York and (more recently)
in London. *(CH)*

International theatre programmes
Gabrielle Enthoven Collection

PERFORMANCE PLACES

When Trevor Nunn, artistic director of the Royal Shakespeare Company, wondered in 1976 'whether the development of theatre architecture isn't going to be killed off by the fire service', he knew that the chances were slim of the Royal Shakespeare Theatre, Stratford-upon-Avon, going up in flames like so many theatres in previous centuries, and being rebuilt to suit the changing ideas of the RSC.

Only 44 years old, the Stratford theatre had already become out-of-date, since it was conceived in terms of a scenic stage like its Victorian predecessor, which burnt down in 1926. Its narrow proscenium arch constricted the potential acting area, and made it difficult to open up the stage so that actor and audience could have the sense of being together in one room. Nunn remarked: 'theatre people really should know better than to want a house that will last till doomsday'.

Attempts to remedy the situation during the previous 25 years came to a head in 1976, when the Stratford auditorium underwent an astonishing transformation for a proscenium theatre. The twin side-balconies were extended through the proscenium arch and round the back of the stage, so that the arch seemed to disappear and the audience encircled the action. Timber cladding on the balconies consciously recalled Shakespearian stage conditions, with the emphasis not on scenic effect but on the spoken word shared in an intimate theatrical situation. What seemed right in 1976 would seem less so now, for experiment with the physical relationship between actor and audience continues to move with the times. But the possibility of a new theatre is even more remote since the Royal Shakespeare Theatre became a listed building in 1980.

Shakespeare's Globe had no proscenium arch. This was an Italian invention designed to frame scenery arranged in perspective in aristocratic entertainments, and not seen in England until it was introduced at Court in the first half of the seventeenth century. In the circular Globe theatre the stage thrust into the centre of the audience like its close relative the portable booth stage (No. 92). Constructed in 1599 with the timbers from the very first purpose-built English playhouse, The Theatre (1576), the Globe probably incorporated recent advances in theatrical architecture: certainly its stage provided a model for that of the Fortune theatre, built in 1600. Shakespeare's fellow-actors did not have to wait long to update the Globe architecture, for in 1613 it burnt down during a performance of *Henry VIII* (one spectator having his breeches extinguished with 'bottle ale'). It was not until after the Restoration in 1660, when most of the Elizabethan theatres had been abandoned, or torn down by the Commonwealth authorities, that English playhouses were designed to accommodate movable scenery, arranged in perspective. The result was a typically English compromise: the old thrust stage was retained for the main action, but now with scenes displayed behind. During the eighteenth century, however, the forestage was gradually cut back, and the action thus 'framed' by the proscenium arch.

The fact that there are no surviving English theatres dating from before the mid-eighteenth century is partly due to the vulnerability of theatres to fire, but it also reflects the readiness with which theatres were knocked down and rebuilt, or altered. Of the early theatres that have survived, the Georgian Theatre at Richmond, North Yorkshire, built in 1788, is the best preserved (No. 95). Disused as a theatre from 1848 it escaped the kind of alterations that modified the original fabric of older buildings such as the

Theatre Royal, Bristol (1766), which remained in active theatrical service.

The frequency with which theatres are put to all kinds of uses is also striking. For instance, the Royal Amphitheatre, Holborn (No. 97), was by turns a circus (twice), a theatre (twice), a skating rink, and a boxing stadium. The Lyceum (No. 96), built as a music hall, is now a Mecca dance hall regularly used for pop concerts. And the Music Hall, Aberdeen, is used weekly by the Christadelphians, a religious sect which forbids smoking, drinking – and theatregoing.

There is also a tradition of converting existing buildings to theatrical purposes, stretching back to the strolling players who performed in banqueting halls, barns, and inn-yards. This practice has recently reasserted itself in striking conversions such as the Royal Exchange Theatre, Manchester, housed in a former cotton exchange (No. 98), The Mermaid Theatre, London (a converted warehouse), the Roundhouse, London (an engine shed), St. Georges Theatre, London (a church), and in the temporary conversion of a sports stadium such as Wembley for pop concerts (No. 99).

The takeover of non-theatrical buildings for performances reflects the modern trend towards architectural design which enables different spaces and performer-audience relationships to be created anew for every play. This demand makes it hard for an architect to create a theatre that is both adaptable and has an identity of its own. One successful solution is the Octagon Theatre, Bolton, which has three stages in one (No. 100). The auditorium can be rearranged to suit an open-ended stage, a thrust stage, or theatre-in-the-round, with seating for 320 to 420. Although the theatre lacks a proscenium arch, quite elaborate sets can be used and changed by means of a revolve.

Another solution is to have three separate auditoria, as at the National Theatre, which between them cater for stage conditions of the past and allow for present experiment. The National houses the Olivier Theatre (seating 1,160), which has an open stage with scenic capability; the Lyttelton (seating 890), with its flexible proscenium stage; and the small Cottesloe, the least defined architecturally, an adaptable studio accommodating 200 to 400. The National Theatre also has what its architect, Denys Lasdun, envisaged as a 'fourth theatre', in the form of the terraces and foyers where people can meet, eat, and drink and watch informal 'platform' performances.

As part of the South Bank arts complex, the National Theatre has a monumental quality which the Pompidou Centre in Paris (No. 101) has avoided by creating an effect of the transient and ephemeral. Its externalized escalators, pipework, and scaffolding-like superstructure give it an inside-out, almost makeshift appearance. Although it does not contain a permanent theatre as such, it provides the backdrop for one, as its forecourts provide a natural site for performances by jugglers, acrobats, and fire-eaters, as also do the buildings that line Venice's Piazza San Marco (No. 92) or the Grande Place of Brussels (No. 91).

Instead of the audience coming to a permanent building, the theatre can go out and seek audiences for itself: thus, the Bubble Theatre (No. 103) shifts its tent-space around the parks of Greater London like a circus or fairground. Existing meeting-places such as pubs and clubs may contain rooms suitable for theatrical events. And street theatre now finds a natural venue in the busy precincts of Covent Garden (No. 104), where Samuel Pepys watched puppet shows over 300 years ago: if its Royal Opera House remains the home of the most stylized of performing arts, its refurbished marketplace has once more become a focus for the most informal of entertainments. *(JF)*

The Nativity Car was one of the ten pageant-wagons used in the 'Ommeganck', an outdoor procession held annually from 1359 or earlier to commemorate the transportation of a miraculous image of the Virgin from Antwerp to Brussels. The wagons carried *tableaux vivants* of biblical scenes (e.g. 'The Annunciation'; 'Christ among the Doctors'), or allegorical scenes from classical mythology (e.g. 'Diana'; 'Apollo and the Nine Muses'), and the procession ended in a service at the church dedicated to the Virgin. The celebration of 31 May 1615 illustrated here is sometimes known as 'Isabella's Triumph', because one wagon represented the Archduchess Isabella and her ladies as a tribute to Isabella as ruler of the Spanish Netherlands.

As in the English medieval mystery cycles, the trades guilds undertook the provision of splendid pageant-wagons. This Nativity Car was almost certainly built by the carpenters, one of whom can be seen miming his craft at the front of the cart. Mary and Joseph are represented probably by citizens in costume. The wagon displays a curious stable of rustic brickwork with rich Corinthian columns supporting a humble thatched roof, surmounted by an angel. It carries live animals and is draped with handsome material.

The Renaissance habit of mixing religious and mythical subjects can be seen in the dragon in the background, ridden by the child of a prominent citizen. James Laver claims in his account of 'Isabella's Triumph' that the dragon is a real camel disguised in an ornate orange and gold skirt, but this is not certain.

The audience is clearly divided between the crowd, who line the square, and the affluent, who watch from the upper windows of houses which are hung with greenery in honour of the occasion. This fusion of religious festival, political propaganda, carnival, circus, and drama was a civic occasion which involved the whole community. *(JS)*

Grande Place, Brussels. Detail from 'The Triumph of
Isabella' in the Ommeganck (1615)
Denis van Alsloot
Oil on canvas 1170 × 3810
V & A: Paintings Department [5928–1859]

The Piazza San Marco is a natural site for theatrical events. Its balconies provide a superior vantage point, like the upper windows overlooking the pageant procession in Brussels on the previous page. Here, however, is not a formal civic occasion but a performance improvised by travelling comedians in the commedia dell'arte tradition which was starting to decline by the date of the engraving, 1762. The performance is taking place in the north-eastern corner of the piazza, the traditional spot for such entertainments, and would have required a licence. Performances took place in the morning and afternoon, and lasted up to two hours. The clock and the long shadows confirm that this is the late afternoon.

On stage in the detail below are some of the stock characters of the commedia dell'arte: Arlecchino on the left is in his chequered suit, next to him the Lady or Serving-Maid, and on the far right Scaramuccia, dressed in his traditional black, and playing a musical instrument. The figure addressing the informal gathering is possibly the Lover, who excelled at rhetoric and wore fine clothes; he may also be doubling as the Prologue.

The action takes place on a portable wooden 'bench' at least five feet high, which appears to have no means of ascent. Contemporary records reveal that the acrobatic skill of the players enabled them to leap on and off the stage at will; this might account for other commedia characters seen mingling with the audience – near the stage a *zanni* with his back to us is bantering with the crowd.

The performance was announced by a parade of the costumed actors through the streets, carrying their stage and property-box, a kind of adaptable trunk on legs, which is just visible on the left at the back of the stage. The curtain, showing a pastoral scene hastily sketched in charcoal or painted in the manner of a woven tapestry, masks a shallow changing booth behind.

The actor could make his entrances and exits by pushing the curtain aside at one end, as is clearly demonstrated in Callot's commedia dell'arte etchings (No. 5). One scene could be rapidly substituted for another, especially if the audience became restive, as in Andreini's scenario *La Schiavetto*, described by K. M. Lea: 'A taste of this comedy is enough, and the audience demand a pastoral instead. Over the curtain for comedy . . . another cloth painted to represent a wood and a flowery field is lowered; the change does not please . . .'. *(JS)*

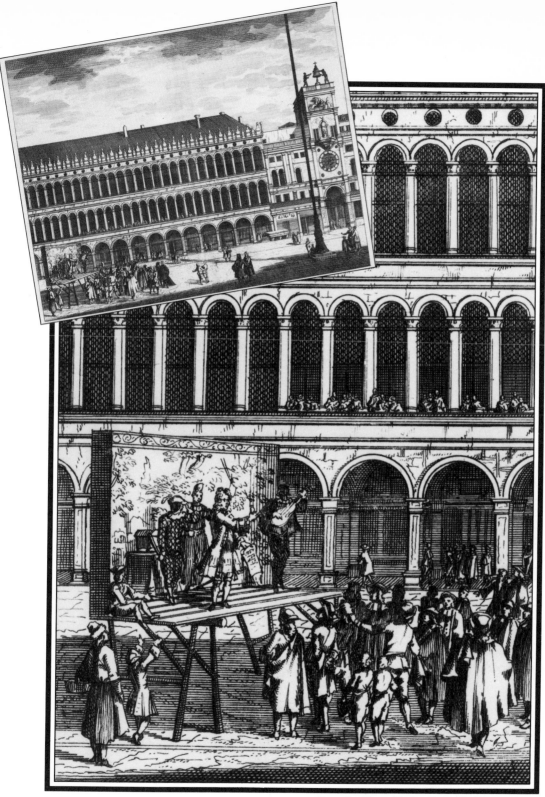

Piazza San Marco, Venice: Commedia dell'arte
performance, 1762
J. Goeree after H. Eland
Engraving 279 × 360
Harry R. Beard Theatre Collection. f.126–27

Detail of the stage performance

Founded in 1935 by Angus L. Bowmer, the Oregon Shakespearean Festival in Ashland is the oldest American festival of its kind and has continued to flourish among an increasing number of rivals: in 1981 there were 36 in the USA alone. The growth in Shakespeare festivals complements that 'passion for building replicas of the Globe Theatre [which] seems to be a distinctly American phenomenon', as Glen Loney and Patricia MacKay observe in *The Shakespeare Complex* (1975).

Little is known for certain about the design of the most famous Elizabethan theatre, the Globe, built in 1599. Being framed of timber, it was probably polygonal rather than round, three storeys high with two stairtowers, and had two main exits. Above the stage was a hut-like structure roofed with thatch like the surrounding galleries, the rest of the auditorium lying open to the weather.

The Elizabethan Stagehouse shown here avoids direct identification with the Globe, since its dimensions are based on the builder's contract for the Fortune theatre erected in 1600 by Peter Streete, who built the Globe in the previous year. The Fortune literally copied many Globe features including the stage which was 43 feet wide and thrust 27 feet 6 inches into the centre of the yard. The major difference between the two was that the auditorium of the Globe was circular while the Fortune's was square.

At Ashland only the section incorporating the stage has been built, with seating for 1,200 disposed in a single fan-shaped tier around the stage – a very different arrangement from Elizabethan theatres, where up to 3,000 people stood round the stage and sat in the galleries. Two large lighting gantries enable plays to be performed in the evening rather than solely in the afternoon, as in Shakespeare's outdoor theatre. Overhead, supported by two pillars, is the superstructure housing the machinery for flying down gods and thrones. Just beneath this is a second-floor gallery, and below the gallery are the upper and lower 'inner stages'.

These small proscenium stages reflect the theories of J. C. Adams, whose book *The Globe Playhouse* (1942) influenced many latter-day 'Globes'. Because of the difficulty of seeing what was going on in these inner stages, Ashland's designer, Richard Hay, later added a balcony which projects in front of the inner stage on the first floor, and created a new entrance to the main stage out of the inner stage below. The inner stage below can still however be put to scenic effect, as in this production of *Doctor Faustus* (1979) showing Faustus's study.

Ashland will soon have a new rival in Detroit, where a 'Third Globe' is to be reconstructed to designs of C. Walter Hodges, based on the Second Globe (1614); and also in London, when Sam Wanamaker builds Richard Hosley's version of the First Globe near its original site on Bankside. *(JF)*

Elizabethan Stagehouse built 1959, Ashland, Oregon. USA
Photograph by Hank Kranzler

The *intermezzo* illustrated opposite was part of a comedy, *La Liberazione di Tirreno e d'Arnea*, performed on 6 February 1617 in honour of the wedding of Ferdinando Gonzaga and Caterina de' Medici. It took place in the private theatre created for the Grand Duke Francesco de' Medici by Buontalenti (1536–1608) in 1586 out of a hall situated beneath the art gallery – the vantage point of the figures in the foreground.

The vast hall measured approximately 87 by 32 metres, seating up to 5,000 on richly carpeted steps, or *gradi*, which lined the hall on three sides. The stage was nearly 23 metres deep, and gave an unimpeded view as it stood 5.5 metres above the floor of the auditorium, which inclined towards it. Ramps led down from the stage, allowing the performers to come forward into the auditorium where they danced in front of (and then with) the guests.

Giulio Parigi designed the settings with assistance from Jacques Callot, who may have been responsible for the costumes. The great depth of the stage is accentuated by Parigi's adherence to the perspective principles of Sebastian Serlio (1475–1554), demonstrated here by his use of rows of trees receding into infinity (probably side shutters which slid in grooves). Centre stage we seen an imposing theatrical machine, a volcanic mountain representing the island of Ischia, in which the monster Typhon is entombed. The mountain belches forth smoke and flames until it bursts open by mechanical means to disgorge a chorus of dancers who descend the ramps to the auditorium.

Above the volcano the gods Jupiter and Mars are lowered in a cloud machine to send down thunderbolts. Their car was hoisted up and down by pulleys, the mechanism being screened by borders above the stage. These ingenious transformations formed the highlight of the performance, as an eye-witness describes: 'this was beautifully staged and several machines were set in motion which made this *intermezzo* a delight to behold.' *(JS)*

PRIMO INTERMEDIO DELLA VEGLIA DELLA LIBERATIONE DI TIRRENO FATTA NELLA SALA DELLE COM
DIE DEL SER.ᵐᵒ GRAN DVCA DI TOSCANA IL CARNOVALE DEL 1616. DOVE SI RAP.ᵛᵃ IL MONTE D'ISCHIA CON IL GIGANTE
TIFEO SOTTO.

Teatro Medici, Uffizi Palace, Florence, 1617
Jacques Callot after Giulio Parigi
Etching cut to 289 × 206
Harry R. Beard Theatre Collection. f.83–11

Richmond typifies the theatres built in small towns by touring circuit companies in the late eighteenth and early nineteenth centuries, but is unique in its state of preservation. Samuel Butler (1750–1812), actor and manager of the 'Yorkshire' circuit, built the theatre in response to the Act of 1788 which restored to local magistrates the power denied them since 1737 to license local performances. He also renewed other houses on his circuit at Harrogate (1788), Kendal (1789), Ripon (1792), Northallerton (1800), and Beverley (1805).

His company would have carried a limited set of stock scenery around their circuit, but new 'wings' were created for the opening of the Richmond Theatre on 2 September 1788 by local artists George Cuitt and Mr. Coatsworth. As Sybil Rosenfeld suggests, these artists may also have been responsible for the decoration of the theatre, traces of which still survive. In 1962 the original colour scheme of Georgian greens was restored and the boxes lined with traditional red canvas, each one bearing the name of a celebrated dramatist.

The theatre is almost rectangular in shape with walls of stone an average of 61 feet long by 28 feet wide. It divides almost equally into auditorium and stage, the auditorium consisting of a gallery with 'kicking boards', upon which audiences would stamp if displeased with a play; a single tier of boxes, three in the middle with four on either side; and a sunken pit that could be floored over for masked balls etc., when the players were not in town. There was a common entrance for all the audience: in Butler's day they paid 3/-, 2/- and 1/- for bench seats in box, pit, and gallery except when a star actor appeared such as Edmund Kean in 1819 and prices rose by up to 50 per cent.

The stage was equipped with footlights which were winched up and down through a slot. Performers entered through proscenium doors flanking the five-feet-deep forestage, which were fitted out to suggest the front doors of houses with balconies above, though as the focus of the action gradually shifted back to the scenic part of the stage actors increasingly made more entrances there. In the front half of the stage were two square traps and a grave trap.

The rear half of the understage was occupied by the theatre's two dressing-rooms. The illustration shows one of these – still used by performers today – with stairs giving access to the back of the stage. The two fires in the dressing-rooms together with one at the rear of the stage were the only source of heating in the building, and there is a record of the theatre being almost empty due to the cold. The auditorium would have been lit by candles which illuminated both stage and auditorium equally.

After the Butler family relinquished the theatre in 1830, various troupes performed there on and off until 1848, when the auditorium was floored over for use as an auction room and the pit demolished to make way for a wine-vault. Serving in turn as a cornchandler's, a furniture store, and, at the start of the last war, a salvage depot, the theatre was eventually restored with the help of modern scholars, particularly Richard Southern, and reopened in 1963. *(JF)*

Georgian Theatre, Richmond, North Yorkshire,
built 1788
auditorium and stage from the gallery
dressing-room below stage
Photographs by Moira Walters

From the time that he took up the management of the Lyceum Theatre in 1878 until his last appearance there in 1902, Henry Irving (see also No. 31) attracted fashionable audiences to witness elaborate productions mounted on a larger stage than that of the 1904 Lyceum shown here. Irving made the fullest use of gas-lighting and limelight effects (see also No. 75), and took the innovatory step of lowering the auditorium lights when presenting realistic scenery and tableaux. Audiences flocked and queued to see Irving's latest stage-pictures just as they did to the Royal Academy. But Irving's Lyceum was almost totally demolished in 1904, to be rebuilt as a music-hall to the design of the architect Bertie Crewe. Opened on 31 December 1904, the new Lyceum boasted the elaborately gilded stucco ornament in Louis Quinze style, characteristic of the overblown type of Edwardian theatre decoration.

By November 1905 the theatre was closed again, and when it reopened under new management in March 1907 it was as a home for popular drama at popular prices. Annual pantomime became an institution, particularly under the Melville family who controlled the theatre from May 1910 until July 1939. Outside, however, the building retained the porticoed entrance of Irving's Lyceum, and this entrance still stands today since war interrupted the plans for the street-widening that threatened its destruction when this photograph was taken in July 1939.

The Melville brothers' management of the Lyceum spanned almost 29 years – longer than any other management there, including Irving's – and under their direction the theatre once more attracted full houses to successful productions, including many melodramas and pantomimes they wrote themselves. When the public enthusiasm for melodrama waned in the 1920s, they presented more varied entertainment: a revue in September 1925, followed by a revival of Shaw's *St. Joan* and a season of Diaghilev ballet in 1926. In 1931 Noël Coward's *Bitter Sweet* transferred to the Lyceum, and later that year Chaliapin appeared in a season of Russian opera. April 1932 saw the elaborate revival of *The Miracle* presented by C. B. Cochran and Max Reinhardt, who converted the interior of the theatre into a Gothic cathedral in a more spectacular way than even Irving could have envisaged.

After the death of Walter Melville in 1937 and of Frederick Melville in 1938, it was announced that the theatre was to be demolished. Following a valedictory production of *Hamlet* in June 1939, with John Gielgud as Hamlet, Fay Compton as Ophelia, and Andrew Cruickshank as Rosencrantz, the theatre's effects were auctioned, and the Lyceum remained empty until 1945, when it was floored over and converted into a dance hall. As such it survives today, with regular pop concerts bringing live entertainment, albeit of a different kind, back to the building once more. *(CH)*

Lyceum Theatre photographed in July 1939
Gabrielle Enthoven Collection

Opening on 25 May 1867, the circus was once more in town – at the Royal Amphitheatre, High Holborn, a building especially designed and erected as a permanent home for equestrian, acrobatic, and dramatic performances. The splendid new amphitheatre was decorated in 'Pompeian style', and lit by 960 gas burners in a crystal sunlight nine feet in diameter. There were comfortable stuffed seats in the pit instead of the usual wooden benches, and sumptuous damask-covered ones in the balcony on the first tier, which ran in front of the private boxes situated underneath the gallery. Behind the pit was a promenade, and in all 2,000 people could be accommodated.

The performances began with a dramatic interlude on the shallow stage, and continued with circus acts in the amphitheatre, during which time the stage area was concealed by a handsome drop-curtain with a classical horse-race scene painted by Julian Hicks. The performer depicted is probably Madame Gerard, the French equestrienne, about to leap from horseback through paper hoops held by assistants. The Amphitheatre boasted two sets of stables and sixteen dressing-rooms, and its publicity material emphasized 'our endeavour to resuscitate . . . the diverting and exciting scenes of the Arena', since 'London has long been without an Equestrian Establishment of any kind whatever'.

Eighty years previously, in 1784, following the success of his outdoor riding school, Philip Astley had constructed a completely covered arena for his equine entertainments, with a built-in stage area for dramatic interludes. The illustration shows the first enclosed amphitheatre, c. 1793, with wooden benches surrounding the sawdust ring, boxes, a stage with a proscenium arch, and an orchestra pit. For this pony race (after a live fox), the stage was extended by ramps into the ring area, and the 'ring-master' can be seen directing the chase.

Astley built three Amphitheatres on the same site in London, each in turn being destroyed by fire. Rebuilding produced increasingly grand interiors with progressively stronger stages to support more horses and even carriages. The third Amphitheatre burnt down in 1841, but the site was purchased by William Batty and the Amphitheatre continued under his ownership and subsequently that of 'Lord' George Sanger until 1893, when the building was condemned. Batty's, Sanger's, and the Holborn Amphitheatres tried to imitate Astley's 'peculiar mixture of elegance and vulgarity', but by the late 1860s the combination of circus and drama had lost much of its appeal. *(CH)*

Royal Amphitheatre, High Holborn, from a
reproduction in *The Illustrated Times*, 22 June 1867
Anonymous
Engraving cut to 248 × 249
Gabrielle Enthoven Collection

**Astley's Royal Grove and Amphitheatre Riding
House, Westminster Bridge Road,** *c.* 1793
Anonymous
Engraving 116 × 186
Gabrielle Enthoven Collection

Like a space module, a theatre has landed within the Great Hall of the Royal Exchange, Manchester. The 100-ton steel and glass structure makes no concessions to the imitation marble pillars and majestic domes of its neoclassic host. The architects, Levitt Bernstein Associates, and designer Richard Negri have created an uncompromising new theatre within an old building. As David Levitt, one of the architects, said: 'The beginning for us was a small paper and wire model on a table, with Richard Negri pacing round it talking about the form of a rose. How, we wondered, would we ever bring this man down to earth? Fortunately, we never have.'

Once the hub of the world's cotton-trading business, Manchester Royal Exchange was built in 1809, and extended and reconstructed in 1874, when its Great Hall was called 'the largest room in the world'. Having suffered extensive damage during the Second World War, the Royal Exchange was rebuilt on a smaller scale in 1953, but still with a Great Hall capacious enough to enclose Manchester Cathedral. The last day's cotton trading took place on 31 December 1968, and the Hall was then unoccupied until it became the permanent home of Manchester's '69 Theatre Company, who secured a lease on the Hall in 1972. After using it during the 1973 Manchester Festival, their temporary tent-like structure was dismantled and work began on constructing the present theatre which opened on 15 September 1976.

Climbing the steps of the Royal Exchange, the audience enters the Great Hall through the imposing portico and is confronted by the circular theatre module within. As Michael Elliott, the artistic director, said: 'The experience of seeing the building as you enter cannot be prepared for, or photographed. It is a place, and places, like people, have to be met.' Passing through the area surrounding the drum of the theatre that is used as a foyer, the audience sees items of stage props and furniture that are to be used during the performance, for there is no conventional backstage area or 'wings', and the actors await their cues in the foyer, making their entrances through the same doors used by the public.

The stage is thus a continuation of the parquet flooring of the Hall, and dramatic sound and lighting effects can be achieved by using the area surrounding the auditorium: 'storms' may be created to reverberate around the spectators, and 'ships' may approach with their twinkling lights visible when the curtains of the clear glass module are drawn back. The lanterns, rigging and flying bars, and the lighting and sound controls are in full view of the audience. As Michael Elliott explains: 'We wanted to explode the artificial mystique that segregates actor and audience. The spectators are so close to the actors that there can be no room for pretence, not even for a second. The emotional content must be real, otherwise the actor must fail. . . . Acting becomes a question of being rather than doing.' *(CH)*

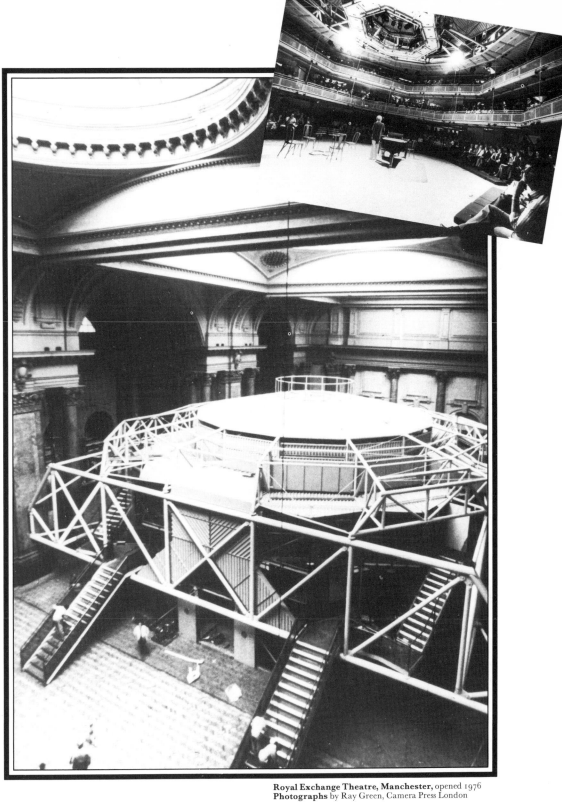

Royal Exchange Theatre, Manchester, opened 1976
Photographs by Ray Green, Camera Press London

Designed by Sir John Simpson and Maxwell Ayrton, and built in 1922 to co-incide with the British Empire Exhibition, Wembley Stadium has come to be regarded as the home of British soccer. However, there are still no purpose-built auditoria in Britain that can hold a crowd of 100,000, although there exists a large following that wants to hear rock music *en masse*, preferably outside. Perhaps it is artificial to view a concert at Wembley Stadium as an extension of the days of the great outdoor festivals of the late 1960s, but there remains a certain nostalgic thrill in a performance at the mercy of the elements, in a building that is an enclosed field.

But converting a football stadium into a concert hall is an immense task. 'The Who and Friends' concert in August 1979 illustrated here (showing The Stranglers in performance) was additionally complex. A special water supply for the laser light show had to be piped in, a stage built, and a crowd control barrier erected across the greyhound track. Fencing round the pitch had to be removed, a dressing-room constructed, conforming with fire regulations, and because of the higher proportion of women expected than for football matches, extra toilets had to be installed. Finally the pitch was covered with tarpaulins and the edges sealed. And all this had to be done in a week.

As no police were to be (officially) on duty inside the stadium, safety and security were other worries. Seven hundred stewards were hired, the majority being stationed on the pitch in teams, and their leaders kept in radio contact with a control room high in the press gallery. Audio-monitors enabled local complaints about noise levels to be speedily checked. Air traffic control and the police were warned about the laser light show – and in case the sound and lights got out of hand, the Wembley engineers were prepared to pull out the plugs.

Afterwards everything had to be dismantled and the sports facilities restored. Was it all worth it? For many of the fans who came it was their first chance in three years to see The Who in London. Inevitably in a such a large auditorium it was difficult to achieve intimate contact with the audience, and the concert thus became something of a ritual, albeit a spectacular one. For many bands, the exigencies of recording contracts, super-tax, and international tours mean that only a limited amount of time is available each year for performances in Britain, and colossal sites such as Wembley Stadium are thus the only option if ticket demand is to be satisfied. *(DF)*

Wembley Stadium: The Stranglers in performance,
1979
Photograph by Robert Ellis

Three theatres in one. A theatre in the round with 420 seats, a theatre with an open-end stage, seating 320, and a theatre with a thrust or three-sided stage, seating 334: all these can be created within the Octagon Theatre, Bolton, one of the first purpose-built adaptable theatres in Britain. Through the ingenious design of eight facets of stepped seating, five of which are movable, the auditorium can be arranged to suit the performance, and the set-up is rarely the same for two consecutive productions. Without the limitations imposed by a proscenium arch, the designer has evolved an ideal theatre space containing, as Jonathan Porter described it, 'an acting area to play *on* rather than a boundary to play "within".'

The auditorium feels spacious, and yet there is a sense of intimacy during performance. No seats are further than nine rows from the stage, and actors are acutely aware of the closeness of the audience. Contact is maintained even when the action takes place on upper-stage areas, which can be built on thrust or open-ended stages. These levels can link with the structure of the auditorium, creating acting areas opposite the highest of the raked seats.

Even the 'loges' or small boxes on a level with the lighting box can be used during performance, and intrepid actors have climbed rope ladders to reach them. In *Jack and the Beanstalk* (Christmas 1979), Jack 'climbed' the beanstalk, disappearing from view and reappearing at various points in the theatre until he was speaking through the lighting grid directly above the auditorium. When the Giant 'lost his footing' chasing Jack, an enormous leg was poked through the grid, dangling above the audience to the horrified delight of the children below.

The Octagon Theatre was designed by Geoffrey Brooks, Bolton's Borough Architect, in collaboration with the then director, Robin Pemberton-Billing. Built at a cost of approximately £95,000, it opened in November 1967 – one of the first new post-war theatres in the North of England. The theatre itself is hexagonal, a shape designed for ease and cheapness of construction. The auditorium is an elongated octagon, which provides the best possible sight-lines for the audience when any of the three stage arrangements are in use.

In a central position in the town, the building is open all day. As Robin Pemberton-Billing said: 'a positive effort was made to avoid any suggestion of "preciousness" about the place – any feeling that it was a sacred "cultural" centre'. It is not just a theatre, but a coffee bar, a bar, a lunchtime buffet, an exhibition gallery, and a meeting-place for those who live and work nearby. Plans have been approved for a second, smaller auditorium, primarily to house the Octagon's Children's Theatre project – the audiences of the future for the Octagon. *(CH)*

Octagon Theatre, Bolton, opened 1967
Photographs by Winter and Kidson, Preston

The full title – *Centre national d'art et de culture Georges Pompidou* – is shortened to *Centre Pompidou* if you're French, *The Pompidou Centre* if you're English, *The Pompidoleum* if you're feeling affectionate, or *that excrescence* if you haven't been there. You might still feel like describing it as a 'monstrosity with its guts hanging out' when you *are* there – but be careful, because you're then in danger of being hit about the head and bustled out by any one of the 50,000 people who visit it every day and love it.

In trying to define this building, some liken it to a factory, some to a cathedral. It is neither, although the French probably work harder at their art and worship their culture more than most. It was André Malraux who, as President de Gaulle's Minister of Culture, invented the idea of the Maisons de la Culture: a network of mostly purpose-built arts centres in the main provincial towns of France where every kind of artistic and cultural manifestation would be freely accessible to all. The Pompidou Centre is, in effect, the Maison de la Culture for Paris.

Fortunately, the Centre was designed by two architects of genius – Richard Rogers, an Englishman, and Renzo Piano, an Italian, who won the international competition for its design. The result is triumphant. Within five floors, each with an area of 150 by 50 metres unbroken by pillars, they have given the right form to an infinite possibility of desirable spaces. Thus, the building not only houses the National Gallery of Modern Art, temporary exhibition galleries, performance spaces, cinémas, libraries of books and records, terraces, promenades, and cafés, but is also itself a work of art. Witty and attractive, it gathers in front of it on the Plateau Beaubourg a host of madcap but skilful popular performers: accordionists, acrobats, conjurors, mimes, fire-eaters, string duos, sword-swallowers, flautists, hitch-hikers, pigeons, cats, and the occasional funny tout.

It is a building for our time – impermanent and replaceable, not a shrine but a place (not a palace) of fun. Part factory, part cathedral, maybe, but jollier than either with its vivid paintwork – red, white, and blue outside, lime green inside – plus a transparent escalator tube clinging to the exterior like a space-age big-dipper, zig-zagging its way up to the top, 42 metres above Paris. Like an ocean liner at berth, with engines turning, it tempts 50,000 people a day aboard for a pleasure cruise. It also cost a thousand million francs. *(AS)*

Plateau Beaubourg, Paris. Outside **The Pompidou
Centre** (opened 1977)
Photograph by Sarah Woodcock

The Newcastle Gulbenkian Studio is a small rectangular theatre, 100 feet by 50 feet, with two or three rows of movable seats on three sides and a gallery above enclosing an acting space 30 feet square. This acting area closely resembles that of The Other Place, Stratford-upon-Avon, which was converted into a theatre by the Royal Shakespeare Company. The Gulbenkian was custom-built in 1970, the present gallery being added as a result of the RSC's visits to Newcastle in 1977 and 1978, when it was constructed at the RSC's request and then sold to the Gulbenkian Studio as a permanent feature. At the time of writing, the RSC still uses Newcastle as the base for its visits to the North East, and this enables them to transport whole productions, including sets, from The Other Place without changes.

For a large part of the year, however, the Gulbenkian accommodates touring groups, whose productions are usually geared towards conventional proscenium auditoria such as church halls – and this can cause problems, such as poor sight-lines from the gallery and the sides. The Gulbenkian Studio accommodates up to 200 people depending on how the seating is arranged, with no member of the audience more than six feet from the acting space.

The tradition of intimate studio theatre goes back at least to Meyerhold, who with Stanislavski founded The Theatre Studio in Moscow in 1905, and to Strindberg's Intimate Theatre of 1907. At about the same time in Berlin, Max Reinhardt created the Kammerspiele, whose dark brown walls focused the audiences' attention exclusively on the play. In modern productions the studio audience usually acts as a frame to the action – sometimes on all four sides, often on three as in Di Seymour's design for *Fanshen* (opposite) at the Crucible Studio, Sheffield which reflects the political message of David Håre's play about the process of learning and development after the revolution in China.

Very often the audience has to cross the acting area to reach the seats, and this, together with the proximity of the actors, helps to break down conventional expectations of theatregoing. The proximity between actor and audience often leads to a tension in the relationship: for the audience there is the fear that the action will spill over into their space, or that they might be touched or asked to participate, while the actors feel exposed to a greater extent than on a large, traditional stage.

The growth of studio theatre in recent years has arisen from the desire to experiment with new plays and new techniques, and to awaken in audiences a new awareness of theatregoing. Such experiments influence production techniques in traditional, larger theatres, and in cases where a studio theatre is attached to and supported by a larger theatre, successful productions can transfer to the larger house, reaching wider audiences and justifying their subsidized status at the same time. *(ER)*

Gulbenkian Studio Theatre, Newcastle, built 1970
Photograph by Chris Madge

Design for Studio Theatre: David Hare's *Fanshen*, first
produced at The Crucible Studio, Sheffield, 10 March
1975, by the Joint Stock Theatre Group
Designer: Diana Seymour
Pen and ink, watercolour and chinese white
497 × 650 [S.288–1980]

A bubble is 'a hollow globule formed by a thin film of liquid around an air or gas'. Bubble Theatre is a hollow space for performance formed by a PVC polyester fabric stretched over tubular steel arches. Two of these yellow bubbles or 'tensi-domes', plus two large articulated trailers, two vans, and 37 performers, musicians, and backstage staff, form the Bubble Theatre Company which appears in London parks during the summer months.

Each week the company performs four plays for adults and children in repertoire, acting in the largest 'bubble', which has a seating capacity of 250 and is lit by 50 lights suspended from a free-standing lighting track. The smaller 'bubble' houses the bar and display area, while the dressing-room is the 40-foot trailer. The smaller trailer houses the costumes and stores the props. The box office looks like a sentry box.

Since the company was founded in 1972 by the Greater London Arts Association to bring professional theatre to outer-London boroughs, it has visited 30 of the 32 London boroughs. It may appear in as many as ten parks in one season, and each move means pulling down the bubbles after the Saturday evening performance and packing them and their contents into the vans and trailers. Erecting them at the new site the following day requires ten men and at least twelve hours to accomplish.

Like strolling players, the Bubble Company takes plays to people who might not ordinarily visit an established theatre. As one visitor said, going to the Bubble 'doesn't mean you have got to get dressed up, miss your tea, go to a strange part of London on the tube, and then fork out money'. Tickets to the Bubble are cheap, and the atmosphere is informal.

Within its plastic 'O', the actors perform theatre-in-the-round to their audience, who can sip drinks during the show, sitting at café-type tables close to the stage. The actors make their exits and entrances by the gangways between the audience; the bubble encloses and involves the spectators.

The Bubble Theatre excites the curiosity of those who see it in their local park, and the fenced enclosure with its brightly-lit sign has a circus or fairground atmosphere. Many of the plays involve music, and you can always smell the grass beneath your feet. The actors have to contend with the British weather, walking over muddy ground from the dressing-room trailer – often in the pouring rain, which can be heard beating on the bubble as they say their lines. But everyone involved agrees that the difficulties are worth it. As one actor said simply: 'It's fun. It's fun to work in and it's fun to watch.' *(CH)*

Travelling Theatre. The Bubble Theatre in
Ravenscourt Park, West London, 1980
Photographs by Roger de Wolf

With its chained escapologist and doll-like lady in fishnet tights, the performance illustrated is *Fumbellow Fellini*, presented by the Free Form Road Show at Covent Garden's May Fair, 1975. Combining elements of popular entertainment such as puppets, clowning, magic, and fire-eating, Free Form included both live and recorded music in their shows which were carefully structured yet flexible. They appeared by invitation, usually in towns devoid of local theatre, staging a new show every summer until 1977 when they became an arts trust, solely concerned with community arts projects.

Covent Garden, while an unusual place to find Free Form, is a traditional site for street theatre. Pepys witnessed a performance of Punch's Puppet Theatre there in 1662, and this area is now the only site in London licensed by the Greater London Council for street performance. To obtain a (free) licence, entertainers must first be auditioned by Covent Garden's Community Association, although some make a pitch without a permit – and, of course, unlicensed entertainment happens wherever performers can attract an audience.

Animal acts thus draw crowds outside the Tower of London, and professional buskers play to theatre and cinema queues – captive audiences waiting to attend more orthodox entertainment. Music students supplement their grants by performing in the street during vacations, not unlike the eighteenth-century actors from patent theatres who performed at fairs during the summer months when theatres were closed.

The unlicensed street performer today is legally in much the same position as the strolling players of the past who were outlawed in the sixteenth century as rogues and vagabonds. Fines today usually average about £5 to £10, yet police will often exercise discretionary critical powers and bear with competent performers who are not causing an obstruction, while London Transport have relaxed by-laws forbidding buskers on their premises. If street entertainers continue to be tolerated, talent will increase as will the pleasure they add to city life.

Street theatre is one of the few forms of entertainment that you can sample before paying for it – or not. To quote Lyn Thomas, who conjures and juggles mainly in the streets with an amusing patter in pidgin French: 'On a good day you can earn as much as £30. But it's not always easy. People give you more when the weather's nice because it puts them in a better frame of mind. The standards will improve if more people are allowed to perform. You have to work hard and you have to be good. You don't issue tickets, and people won't give money for rubbish.' *(CH)*

Street Theatre in Covent Garden Piazza, 1975
Photograph by Clive Boursnell

KEY

1. Figure. Macheath in *The Beggar's Opera*, Lyric Theatre, Hammersmith, 1920
2. Figure. Polly Peachum in *The Beggar's Opera*, Lyric Theatre, Hammersmith, 1920
3. Figure. Mother Goose
4. Tee-shirt. Souvenir of Pink Floyd
5. Booklet. Illustrated souvenir of *Much Ado About Nothing*, St. James's Theatre, London, 1898
6. Jug. Commemorating the performances of Joseph Grimaldi
7. Souvenir. Issued on 200th performance of *Monsieur Beaucaire*, Comedy Theatre, London, 1903
8. Cut-out model. Shakespeare's Globe theatre. Designed by Waldo S. Lanchester
9. Clock. Commemorating the performances of Andrew Ducrow
10. Scroll. Commemorating Ellen Terry's Golden Jubilee in the theatre. Theatre Royal, Drury Lane, 1906. Designed by William Nicholson, 1906
11. Wall hanging, overprinted with portraits and lyrics of The Beatles
12. Bowl. Illustrated with acrobatic and equestrian subjects, painted by Thérèse Lessore, c. 1907
13. Bust. Mozart
14. Statuette. Commemorating the release of the album 'Presence' by Led Zeppelin, 1976
15. Match case. Souvenir of 1,000th performance of *Charley's Aunt*, Royalty Theatre, London, 1895
16. Tile. Illustrated with image of *King Lear* Act V sc. iii. Minton. Designed by J. Moyr Smith, 1873
17. Trinket box. Souvenir of the opening of the Royal Alexandra Theatre, Toronto, 1907
18. Postcard. Camille Clifford and Leslie Styles in *Belle of Mayfair*, Vaudeville Theatre, London, 1906
19. Postcard. Lily Elsie in *The Dollar Princess*, Daly's Theatre, London, 1909

20. Postcard. Constance Collier and Herbert Tree in *Nero*, His Majesty's Theatre, London, 1906
21. Postcard. Frank and Constance Benson in *Henry V*, Lyceum Theatre, London, 1900
22. Postcard. Henry Lytton and Clara Dow in *Iolanthe*, Savoy Theatre, London, 1908
23. Postcard. Anna Pavlova in *Chopiniana* in 1908
24. Postcard. Commemorating Ellen Terry's Golden Jubilee in the theatre, 1906
25. Postcard. Tamara Karsavina and Adolph Bolm in *Le Pavillon d'Armide* in 1909
26. Postcard. Sarah Bernhardt. Publicity still
27. Postcard. H. B. Irving in *The Lyons Mail*, Shaftesbury Theatre, London, 1908
28. Postcard. Madge Carr Cook and Louise Closser in *Mrs. Wiggs of the Cabbage Patch*, Terry's Theatre, London, 1907
29. Postcard. Billie Burke. Publicity still
30. Postcard. Lily Elsie. Publicity still
31. Postcard. Basil Gill in *Much Ado About Nothing*, His Majesty's Theatre, London, 1905
32. Cruet set. Modelled as Joseph Grimaldi, c. 1850
33. Statuette. W. S. Penley as Charley's Aunt in *Charley's Aunt*, Royalty Theatre, London, 1892. Designed by Albert Toftse, 1913
34. Plate. Commemorating the acrobatic performances of Jean-Baptiste Auriol
35. Figure. Ellen Terry as Queen Katherine in *Henry VIII*, Lyceum Theatre, London, 1892. Designed by Charles John Noke (Royal Doulton, early 20th century)
36. Cut-out model. Set for *The Beggar's Opera*, Lyric Theatre, Hammersmith, 1920. Set designed by Claud Lovat Fraser
37. Framed Disc. Presented to T. Rex to mark the sale of 250,000 copies of 'Get It On', August 1971

38. Jug. Commemorating the performances of Dan Leno
39. Chocolate box. Illustrated with images from Shakespeare's plays. Rowntree & Co. Ltd.
40. Jug with lid. Modelled as George Robey. Royal Doulton
41. Lavender Bag. Souvenir of *Sweet Lavender*, Terry's Theatre, London, 1888
42. Fan. Souvenir of King's Theatre, London, c. 1796
43. Fan. Souvenir programme of *Fanfare For Europe*, Royal Opera House, Covent Garden, 1973
44. Towel. Souvenir of the appearance of the New York City Ballet at the New York State Theatre, Lincoln Centre, New York, 1979
45. Miniature mug. Illustrated with circus subject
46. Figure. Popov the clown.
47. Horse Brass. Modelled as Shakespeare's cottage at Stratford-upon-Avon
48. Brochure. Pictorial souvenir of *Nero*. Issued to commemorate 50th performance, His Majesty's Theatre, London, 1906. Cover designed by Charles Buchel
49. Brochure. Pictorial souvenir of *Hair*, Shaftesbury Theatre, London, 1968. Brochure designed by Russell/James Associates
50. Brooch. Souvenir of The Beatles in the form of a guitar illustrated with image of Ringo Starr
51. Talcum powder container. Souvenir of The Beatles
52. Plate. Souvenir of The Beatles
53. Pictorial souvenir. Issued in 1895 on the first anniversary of *The Shop Girl*, Gaiety Theatre, London, 1894
54. Travelling Flask. Given by Noël Coward to members of the original cast of *Bitter Sweet*, His Majesty's Theatre, London, 1929